MUSTANG

· T · H · E ·

Enduring Legend

MUSTANG

·T·H·E·

Enduring Legend

GALLERY BOOKS
An Imprint of W. H. Smith Publishers Inc.
112 Madison Avenue
New York City 10016

DEDICATION

To Becky and Ambre, who are my constant inspiration, and a special mention to Jack Dwyer, Gary Miller, Pacific Mustang Club, and Walt Wise, without whose help this book could never have been published.

ACKNOWLEDGMENT

The publishers gratefully acknowledge the invaluable assistance provided by the following individuals and organizations throughout the preparation of this book:

Unique Color Lab, Fort Wayne, Indiana; Bob French; Bill Stroppe Ford, Long Beach, California; Fred Engle; Dave Friend; Bill Martin; John Martino; Gary and Paulette Miller; T. Birds; Elvira and Siegfried Grunze; Grayce and George Klass; Charlotte Brodie and Shy; Ed Monson; Rick Saute; Harold Fredrickson; Al Kropff; Dave Finner; Pacific Mustang Club, Chatsworth, California; Ron Miller; Jack's Camera Shop, Muncie, Indiana; Walt and Marilyn Wise; Skip MacDougal; Robert Pyle; Don Hoyt; Charles Lawrence; Robb Wilcox; Merlin M. Milbaugh; Jim Gilliland; Claude Lafler; Tony Sica; Richard DiLabio; Richard Peratta; Bobby Seals; Gerald, Darlene and Michelle King; Richard Emery.

CLB 2313
© 1989 Colour Library Books Ltd., Godalming, Surrey, England.
This edition published in 1989 by Gallery Books,
an imprint of W.H. Smith Publishers, Inc.,
112 Madison Avenue, New York, 10016
Color separation by Hong Kong Graphic Arts Ltd., Hong Kong.
Printed and bound by New Interlitho.
All rights reserved
ISBN 0 8317 6196 2

Gallery Books are available for bulk purchase for sales promotions and premium use. For details write or telephone the Manager of Special Sales, W.H. Smith Publishers, Inc.,
112 Madison Avenue, New York, New York 10016. (212) 532-6600

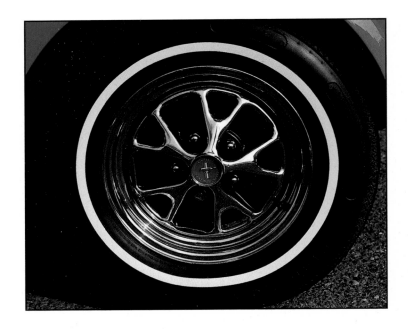

SPECIFICATIONS
1964½–65

		(April 1964–August 1965)	Year production
No.	**Model**		**1965**
63A	Fastback, standard		71,303
63B	Fastback, deluxe		5,776
65A	Hardtop, standard		464,828
65B	Hardtop, deluxe		22,232
65C	Hardtop, bench seats		14,905
76A	Convertible, standard		94,496
76B	Convertible, deluxe		5,338
76C	Convertible, bench seats		2,111
	TOTAL		680,989

Models		**Prices/Weights**
07	hardtop, 6	$2372/2445
07	hardtop, 8	$2480/2720
08	convert, 6	$2614/2669
08	convert, 8	$2722/2904
09	fastback, 6	$2589/2495
09	fastback, 8	$2697/2770

General Specifications	**1964½**	**1965**
Wheelbase:	108.0	108.0
Overall length:	181.6	181.6
Overall width:	68.2	68.2
Standard Trans.:	3 speed manual	3 speed manual
Optional Trans.:	Overdrive 4 speed manual 3 speed automatic	Overdrive 4 speed manual 3 speed automatic

Engine Availability			**1964½**	**1965**
Type	**CID**	**HP**		
I6	170	101	Standard	—
I6	200	120	—	Standard
V8	260	164	Standard	—
V8	289	200	Optional	Standard
V8	289	225	Optional	Optional
V8	289	271	Optional	Optional

INTRODUCTION

Why is it that when one thinks of cars having achieved legendary status, it is always the most expensive exotica that springs to mind – Ferrari or Bugatti, for instance. The more unattainable the car, the more legendary it seems to become.

Actually, there is nothing odd about it. We all have dreams, don't we? At least these cars can justify their legendary status, either through road and track performance, superb and lasting design, even the charisma of their makers, and in some cases, like Ferrari, a combination of all these things. But to most people Ferraris and their like remain a dream – a poster upon a teenager's bedroom wall or a Minimarque 43 model car. So how is it that a common little car like the Mustang is up there with the giants?

When Lee Iacocca became Ford's general manager, he took over a division regarded at best as the one that built the cars Auntie Myrtle liked to drive. Fords sold well enough, but for the burgeoning youth market lumbering Galaxies and economical, compact Falcons did not quite click with the "Surfing USA" image. They looked elsewhere

Although the 289 V8 is synonymous with Mustang, early examples (these and previous pages) were delivered with the smaller 260 (facing page top). Above left: attractive wheel sported the pony emblem in center. Below: transmission was automatic in the majority of Mustangs.

8

for their fun. Lee Iacocca determined to give them what they wanted; his master stroke scribbled in his little black book, waiting for the right time to be let out.

When the soldiers returned home from war, they returned to wives and girlfriends whom they had not seen for three years or more. The result was a massive baby boom – Mother Nature's way of replenishing the species, you might coyly say.

Ford marketing manager Chase Morsey, Jr., noticed the population trend showing up in research data. The statistics predicted that between 1960 and 1970 there would be 11.5 million people in the 15–19 and 20–24 age groups. For Iacocca this was the target area; a market looking for the right car.

Pushing aside Auntie Myrtle, Iacocca introduced Ford's new "Total Performance" program. Galaxies developed muscles and started winning races, while Falcons tore up and down snowy slopes in the Monte Carlo Rally. Meanwhile, back in beautiful downtown Dearborn, market researchers were busily dissecting information obtained from field studies around the country. The findings singled out people in the 16–24 age bracket as the group that spent the most. Furthermore, this group knew what type of car they wanted.

On April 17, 1964, Lee Iacocca gave them the car of their dreams. A car with good looks, a sporting personality and a name that conjured up images of Shane riding into the sunset, of horses galloping across the plains, wild and free. An instant legend was born; the Mustang, like the Model T years before, was a people's car.

As we shall see, the Mustang was an instant success. Everybody wanted one, and those who didn't buy a Mustang in 1964 or 1965 bought one later. It broke all sales records for a new car and even if some of the motoring scribes expressed disappointment, to the general public it was the best thing since "I Love Lucy."

As the right car for the right time, the Mustang had no peer. Its base price was a mere $2,368, yet it conveyed the impression that it cost a lot more. For this you got six cylinders, three speed manual, bucket seats, four wheels and steering. That was about it. Unlike many bare-boned cars, the Mustang still managed a look of class, for which credit must go to the late but great stylist Gene Bordinat. As vice president and director of Ford's styling, his hand was on the tiller throughout the Mustang program. "The Mustang," Bordinat once said, "was the result of one of the most exciting and most satisfying design programs with which I have been connected in my 25 years in automotive styling."

The average Mustang buyer generally opted for more than a base car. For slightly less than $3,200 he or she got a V8, radio, automatic transmission, power steering and power disc brakes, as well as whitewall tires, clock, tachometer, tinted windshield, console, rocker moldings and padded sun visors. This is just a sampling of what the customer's money could buy; the options list was as long as a street block!

The opposition was struck dumb. They had nothing in the works that was remotely like the Mustang. Only Chrysler came close with a sporty fastback, but the Barracuda wasn't in the same league. So taken aback was G.M. that at a private showing for top executives a Mustang was

A beautifully restored 1964½ shows off the good-looking lines that were to appeal to millions.

displayed along with G.M.'s 1965 models as if to say "who's been asleep?"

Points, points, points. Everywhere Mustangs went they scored points. Europeans, often unimpressed with Detroit iron, took to the Mustang almost as enthusiastically as Americans. Even the normally cool British motoring press admired the Mustang, albeit with reservations. Without doubt the most talked about car for several months after its introduction, the Mustang was already becoming a legend. *Car Life* magazine obviously thought so; their 1965 test refers to the car as a "classic", and *Time* magazine went one better in its review when it likened Mustang to a Ferrari for the masses. This was perhaps the best description anybody gave Ford's little "pony."

As time went on many other factors helped cement Mustang's legendary status. Performance in the shape of a fastback GT, bigger, more powerful engines, handling packages, and Carroll Shelby all contributed to the success. And if anything or anyone set the seal on a legend, it was a legend itself. Shelby's involvement lit a fire under the pony

Previous pages: the profile that brought a new term into motoring's vocabulary: the Pony Car. Right: headlight surround on early Mustangs was of an awkward design. Below: the early interior is sparse, although the steering wheel gives a sporty look, even if holes in spokes are fake. Facing page: wire wheel hubs were one of many options available in 1965.

and it turned it into a bucking bronco kicking at the traces.

Camaro, Cougar, Barracuda, Challenger, Javelin – these were some of Mustang's major competitors, most of them just as good, and some maybe a little better. Yet none of them attained the heights of America's original pony car, nor commanded the respect that Mustang enjoys. No matter where you look you are bound to find some reminder of Mustang almost every day.

When we talk of legend, we are really talking 1964½ to

1973. To many, these, the first generation Mustangs, are the only cars worthy of recognition. Certainly they have a panache and individuality not shared with any other make. For a long time none of the clubs would recognize the Mustang II, one of the arguments being that the II shared much with the Pinto. This may be so, and certainly the later Mustang could not be compared to its illustrious forebears, which, incidentally, started life sharing quite a portion of their makeup with the Falcon and Fairlane.

15

The third generation Mustang took to the road in 1979. Its European good looks appealed to many, and the car was picked to pace the Indianapolis 500. Ten years later the same basic front engine, rear drive platform remains, even if the skin has been stretched to hide the middle-age spread. In its GT form, today's Mustang is a true performer that continues to sell well.

Twenty five years have passed since Ford first opened the stable doors. The early Mustangs are collectible, but hardly a day goes by without seeing one or more on the road, and it says something for their durability that even in the Midwest they can survive, although the rear quarter panels may leak like a sieve and the floor pan be virtually non-existent! The author remembers watching a Los Angeles street and counting no fewer than fourteen mid-Sixties Mustangs driving by within the space of just twelve minutes.

Mustang's front engine, rear drive technology is dismissed by some as antiquated, especially in the light of other Ford products. Try the latest Mustang GT and see what *you* think. Even after 25 years the magic is very much all there; the appeal undiminished, the language universal.

As you turn the following pages, you will find Mustangs are as diverse and varied as many of the hand-built exotics. If you are new to Mustang, you will begin to find it habit forming. It always has been and always will be a happy car, an endearing car, the stuff of which legends are made.

CHAPTER 1 1964½ – 1973

Lee Anthony Iacocca had come a long way. Only thirty-six years old, and here he was general manager of Ford Motor Division. Born of Italian parents who ran a successful hot dog restaurant in Allentown, Pennsylvania, Lee became interested in cars when his father added a car rental business to his activities. Perhaps fate took a hand at this point – the rentals were all Fords.

Unable to do military service at the outbreak of the war – he was classed 4F after surviving a severe bout of rheumatic fever – Iacocca studied engineering instead.

Above: pony in corral left no room for mistaking this car; in fact, pony was designed to canter in the opposite direction but a production error had it going this way. Right: whichever way you look at it, the Mustang boasts good proportions.

His efforts rewarded him with a Master's degree and with this in his pocket he had the pick of many openings available at a time when engineers were in short supply. No matter how enticing the offers were, Iacocca decided it was Ford he wanted to work for.

Ford assigned Lee to an eighteen-month training program designed to take promising personnel through every stage of automobile manufacture. Halfway through the program Lee discovered he didn't really want to be an engineer at all. He wanted to go into marketing instead. Leaving Dearborn with a letter of recommendation from Ford, Lee got himself a position in the fleet sales department of a Ford dealership in Chester, Pennsylvania.

By 1949 Iacocca was zone manager, and in 1953 he was promoted to assistant sales manager. His efforts came to the notice of Dearborn after he instigated a special time payments plan in 1956. It was so successful that Robert S. McNamara, one of the original Ford "whizz kids" and now vice president of Ford Division, made Iacocca's payments scheme part of Ford's marketing strategy.

The next few months could be described as a blur for Lee Iacocca. He married Mary McLeary, was posted to Washington, D.C. as district manager for the area and just as he and his wife were preparing to move, he was summoned to Dearborn. When he emerged from the meeting, Lee A. Iacocca was Ford's new national truck marketing manager.

Naturally he made a success of the job, and a year later became head of car marketing. He was so good at his work that in 1960 Ford promoted him to head both truck and car marketing.

And here he was, Lee Anthony Iacocca, one-time car salesman, now general manager of the mighty Ford Division, replacing Robert McNamara, who became president of Ford on November 10th 1960.

The difference between the two men was enormous: one a conservative introvert, always taking the safe road; the other outspoken, never afraid to take chances, his credo that motoring should be fun. Under Iacocca's direction Ford took the yellow brick road and eventually everyone else followed suit.

Ford placed a lot of reliance on market research – it helped create the Thunderbird and Falcon as well as the Edsel, the $250 million flop Ford executives liked to pretend had never happened. Regarded as the worst market research blunder since the "Dewey defeats Truman" debacle, Ford tried to justify the Edsel fiasco by claiming that the market was there but the timing was wrong.

"We have market research going on all the time, full blast", said Iacocca in an interview about the Mustang, adding that they had experts who watched every change in customers' whims, monitored graduation figures, and even kept track of the number of repossessions. Then came the answer as to why the Mustang.

"We had been aware," Iacocca went on, "that an unprecedented youth boom was in the making. The population was growing fast … the 16–24 age group was growing even faster." Young people were now earning more, they were better educated and had more independence than ever before. The survey found that they knew exactly what they wanted, and it wasn't a full-size Galaxie or compact Falcon. What the country's youth really wanted was a sporty car with four seats and a trunk; a car very similar to the idea Lee Iacocca had scribbled in his little black book. With the surveys and his own intuition,

Ford celebrated Mustang's first birthday with the GT (these and previous pages). In reality an option package, the GT Equipment Group transformed the standard Mustang with grille-mounted fog lamps (above), GT emblems, handling package and body stripes. Beware imitation GTs, though, they're out there waiting to take you to the cleaners! The GT also boasted real holes, rather than painted indentations, in the steering wheel spokes (facing page).

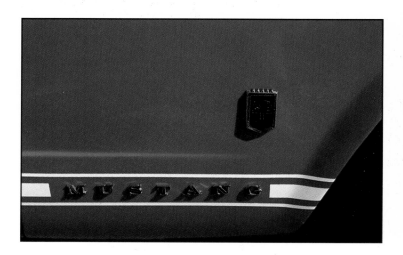

Lee was convinced he was right. He started to voice his ideas, and in 1961 he and a group of Ford high fliers began to meet at the Fairlane Inn in Dearborn to thrash out ideas. The members of the Fairlane Committee – as they called themselves – agreed unanimously with Iaccoca about the sort of car that was needed.

Gene Bordinat, Ford's styling chief, engineer Herb Misch, and former Aston-Martin product planner Roy Lunn, put together a very advanced package based upon what had been gleaned from the market research, adding their own unique interpretation to create one of the most advanced design concepts Ford had ever undertaken.

Although officially referred to as the T-5 Project , the trio that gave it life christened it the Mustang I. Its wind-splitting design was very low, aerodynamic and radical. It used a

German-built V4 derived from Ford's Taunus 12/15M, and all-round independent suspension with variable rated springs and shocks. A four-speed transaxle with cable-operated gear linkage was modified from Ford's ill-fated fwd Cardinal project. Other bits and pieces, including the disc/drum breaking system, were taken from Ford of Britain's Consul. A multi-tubular space frame with stressed aluminium outer panels made up the body, which weighed a mere 1,148 pounds, yet the design provided the strength of a ten ton truck. A pretty advanced package, all things considered.

Troutman and Barnes of California were commissioned to build this radical vehicle in time for showing at the United States Grand Prix at Watkins Glen. Why an outside builder? Strange as it may seem, Ford was not equipped to put together a vehicle as special as the Mustang.

It was a clever ploy to unveil the car at Watkins Glen. If you want publicity, go to a racetrack, because everybody, including the world's motoring press, will be there. Just before the Grand Prix in October 1962, Ford pulled the wraps off the prototype.

Racing personalities such as Dan Gurney and Stirling Moss drove the Mustang I several laps around the track

Facing page, from top: all early V8-powered Mustangs carried identification emblems such as this; six-cylinder models, however, didn't get one. Attractive standard wheel has five lugs. GTs had ID behind front wheel arch. If you're prepared to pay the price, you too can have individual license plate. Above: 1965 Mustang profile looks right in every respect.

and came away shaking their heads in disbelief. They thought the car too good to be true, and the motoring press went crazy over it. Reacting to rumors that the car was destined for full production, correspondents heaped praise on Ford for having the courage of its convictions – or to put it simply, for taking the American Motor industry where it had never gone before.

Unfortunately it was a leap that never quite happened, and was actually dismissed by lacocca long before it left the design studios. "… it can't be a volume car. It's too far out," Lee is reported to have said.

Although the motoring hacks bleated and banged their heads against their typewriters, most simply did not understand that, as a volume car, the Mustang I in its

Previous pages: park ranger and her horse, Shy, make an ideal backdrop for the beautiful '66 convertible Below: when is a wire wheel not a wire wheel? The optional Mustang hubcap has an expensive look. Bottom: the steering wheel boss lets you know you're driving a Mustang. Right: simpler grille identifies this Mustang as a '66; note pony's corral no longer has bars but is floating free.

present form just could not be. Dearborn's existing mass production technology was not geared for space frames and aluminum. Besides, it would have been prohibitively expensive to produce, thus defeating Iacocca's objective – that of producing an inexpensive sports type car, perhaps similar to the classic 1955–1957 Thunderbird, but with room for an extra two passengers.

Meetings between engineers, designers, Iacocca and the Fairlane group went on day after day. Finally, agreement was reached and the designers went away with the engineers, both groups pondering this brief: a car stretching a maximum 180 inches overall, weighing no more than 2,500 pounds, having four bucket seats and making use of existing Falcon and Fairlane components to help keep the cost down to a projected $2,500.

To get the best input of creative ideas, Iacocca suggested holding a competition between the Ford studios. Four studios were selected, each given Iacocca's brief and told to produce at least one model containing all the necessary requirements. Clays had to be ready for viewing inside three weeks!

A tall order to say the least, but the task was completed in the allotted time. Working round the clock, the stylists at the four studios produced a grand total of seven clays and on August 16th, 1962, Iacocca, Fairlane Committee members and designers unanimously agreed on one model.

It was called Cougar and had been designed by Dave Ash, who was assistant to Joe Oros, Ford's design studio chief. The name was chosen because it was felt that the design had a lithe, cat-like look, although this was dropped in favor of Mustang. Whilst the names Mustang I and Mustang II (as Ash's winning design was called) were being used at the time, it had not been chosen as the model name for the eventual production car.

Now they had the design, Iacocca's next task was to convince Ford top brass that there was a real need for the car. It required all Lee's powers of persuasion to convince a group that had already committed funds for major retooling of the 1965 models to look at the project. They listened and were even quite optimistic, but before they could make up their minds they wanted a full study of Lee's proposals. Then Henry Ford II stepped in. He looked at the clays and liked what he saw. On September 10th, 1962, word came down that Project T-5 had been given the go-ahead. Launch date was set for April 17th, 1964.

That a car could go from a stylist's clay to full production in eighteen months does not sound possible, but in the Mustang's case a lot of the major work had already been done. For one thing only slight modifications were carried out to Dave Ash's design, and then it was a simple case of engineering the body to fit Ford Falcon/Fairlane components. Chasis, suspension, driveline and dashboard instruments came from Falcon, while Fairlane provided the engines. Using proven off-the-shelf parts simplified production and saved a great deal of money, the savings eventually handed on to the customer in the form of a $2,500 price tag. Only one thing remained to be solved: Project T-5 needed a name. In retrospect it seems utterly crazy; there was the name, Mustang, staring them in the face. It had even been used on the prototypes. Yet Ford called in their advertizing agency, J. Walter Thompson, to

Right: this rear three-quarter view of the '66 convertible shows well designed taillights. Although these appear to be six individual lights, they in fact consist of a single piece of red plastic covered by a die cast molding.

look for a suitable name. As Lee Iacocca had a preference for animal names, the agency went to Detroit's Public Library and selected six, including Mustang.

It is probably thanks to the agency men, whose job it is to conjure images in the public's eye, that the name Mustang was finally chosen. When the Ford men thought of Mustang, they thought of the WWII fighter aircraft. The last thing they wanted to project was a war-like image, but J. Walter Thompson changed all that with romantic visions of wild ponies galloping across the prairie; of cowboys riding into the sunset. Described in this way the Mustang name sounded good, and so it was chosen.

March 9, 1964, and the very first production Mustang rolled off the assembly line. It was a white coupé with red interior and a 260-cubic-inch V8 under the hood. Eventually an airline pilot, Captain Stanley Tucker of Newfoundland, Canada, would buy Number One, which now resides proudly at the Henry Ford Museum in Dearborn, Michigan.

By now everybody knew something was cooking at Ford. *Motor Trend's* rumor mills had been plugging away at it for months and no doubt selected pieces of information had been "leaked" by the company. As launch day neared, media attention had been whipped up to fever pitch. Then, a week or so before the Mustang was unveiled, both *Time* and arch rival magazine *Newsweek* ran cover story

To celebrate the sale of one million Mustangs, Ford put out a limited edition model called the Sprint (these and previous pages). Even though it was mechanically identical to any other six-cylinder Mustang, at least it came with a chrome air cleaner and special engine decal which read "Mustang powered Sprint 200." Below: the steeply raked windshield allows for only a narrow vent window. Right: lack of a phony rear scoop adds to the lines of an otherwise appealing car.

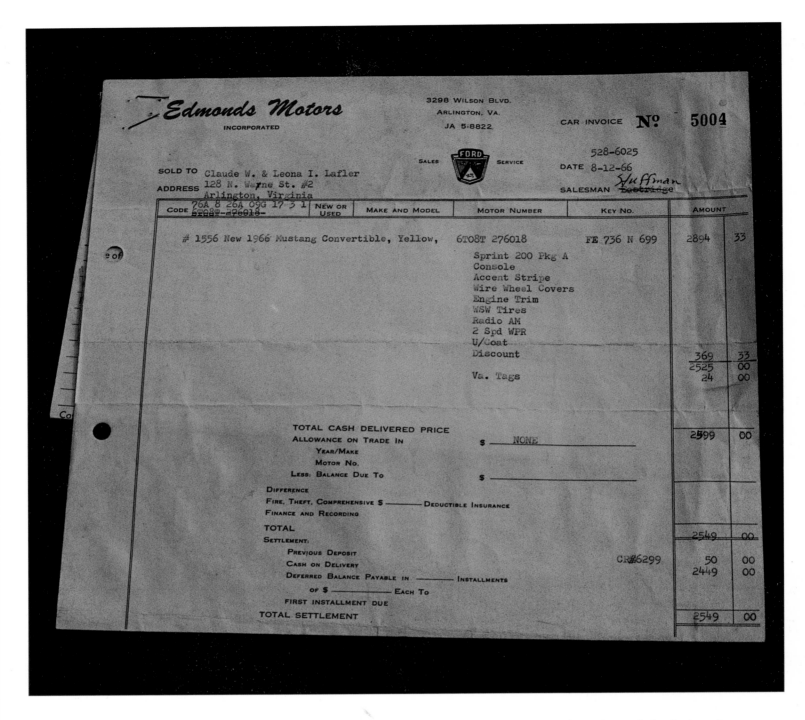

features on Iacocca and the car. The people at *Time* were not amused; they had been in on the secret since the early days of Mustang II and had had a photographer on hand to follow the Mustang through to launch day. How *Newsweek* managed it nobody's saying.

Because public interest was so high Ford chose the New York World's Fair as a suitable setting for the launch, making sure the world's media would be there to record the event. As the great day approached, Mustangs were spirited into Ford dealerships nationwide, past the eyes of little boys eager to get a glimpse of the car everyone was talking about.

Launch day dawned and excitement was at fever pitch. Not since who knows when had a nation been engulfed in such mass hysteria over a motor car. Had alien beings landed in the middle of New York that fine spring day of April 17th, 1964, nobody would have known – or probably cared; America had gone to the Ford dealership to see the Mustang.

It has been estimated that 4 million Americans visited Ford dealerships that day. In Garland, Texas they sold out so fast that 15 people bid on the last Mustang in the showroom. To protect his car, the eventual winner slept in it

while his check was being cleared. And almost everyone has heard of the truck driver who was so mesmerized by what he saw that he accidentally drove his truck straight through the dealer's showroom window! By day's end all available Mustangs were gone and more than 22,000 retail orders had been taken across the country.

Even Ford was taken aback by the public's reaction. That the Mustang would do well was never in doubt, but the scale of the response was more than had been bargained for. Only the Dearborn assembly plant had been geared for Mustang production, at a capacity of 1,300 units a day. Demand for the car was so strong that a second plant in San Jose, California was transferred to Mustang production in July, thereby increasing capacity to 1,800 units a day. This still was not enough as a demand continued to exceed expectations, so Ford converted its

Above: $2,549! Those were the days. As a Sprint's original invoice shows, one got a lot of car for the money. Today, that sum would just about pay for a new Mustang's rubbery steering wheel! Facing page top: the dash is simplicity itself and completely functional. Facing page bottom: it looks bigger than it really is; the tire shows the limited depth of the Mustang's trunk.

34

plant at Metuchen, New Jersey, to take up the slack. By 1965 Mustang production capacity had increased to 50,000 units a month.

But what of the car that had turned a nation on its head? One look at the Mustang said it all. It was cute. It was fun. It had a winning personality. Most importantly, it was affordable, its base price of $2,372 putting the Mustang within easy reach of even high school students working part time at the local gas station. Moreover, it had a list of options as long as the Mississippi, enabling the buyer to tailor his or her model to suit their own individual demands.

Although the Mustang was launched in April 1964, it was officially a 1965 model. In its first 16 months it broke all existing records, selling 680,969 units. In fact over 100,000 were sold in the first four months alone! It was a triumph of design which met Lee Iacocca's original guidelines almost exactly. Wheelbase was 108 inches, overall length 181.6 inches, height 51.1 inches. Base power was provided by a 170-cubic-inch overhead valve straight six, with a 260-cubic-inch V8 as an option. Also on the options list was Ford's excellent 289-cubic-inch V8. Standard with all engines was a three speed manual transmission, although most folk opted for the four-speed manual or three-speed Cruise-O-Matic.

Of the three original engine options offered, none survived beyond autumn 1964. The Falcon 170 cid six was dropped in favor of the 200 cid six normally found in Fairlanes, while the 260 cid V8 was discontinued entirely and replaced by a 2 bbl 289 V8 developing 195 bhp (later to be raised to 200 bhp). Finally, the initial 289 developing 210 bhp was replaced because its compression ratio was too low. In its place came an updated 289 developing 225 bhp. Although it had been promised earlier, the special High Performance 289 V8 did not become available until late June. Rated at 271 bhp, this engine proved it was no dowager duchess, hurtling the Mustang to over 120 mph. That was respectable in the days when the answer for more power was more cubic inches which, as we shall see, Mustang was soon to push under the hood.

No doubt about it, Mustangs were certainly good-looking cars. Not quite as *bon vivant* as the 1955–1957 Thunderbirds perhaps, but attractive with excellent proportions whichever way the car was viewed. Ford's director of styling once put it this way: "It is as close as we know how to come in designing a car that has the emotional appeal of good styling without the added expense attendant to Thunderbird luxury. I like to think of it as the car for the masses with styling for the elite."

A hardtop coupé and a convertible were the only two body styles available when the Mustang first appeared. In profile, the car had a lithe look which was accentuated by the sharply sculptured sides allied to the long hood and short, kicked up rear – a theme that was rapidly becoming the fashion in automotive styling.

At the front, a simple honeycomb grille was recessed behind twin chrome bars joined at the center by a horizontal opening called a corral. The reason for this description is obvious: the corral contained the galloping pony that was to become as famous as Ferrari's Prancing Horse. The sides and bottoms of the grille were framed by a slender chrome band, while three simulated air ducts flanked either side.

In the days when the police didn't bother so much about handing out speeding tickets, Carroll Shelby's GT350 Mustang derivative (these and previous pages) meant fast, furious fun on the highways and byways of America. Ford wanted Mustang to have a sportier image and Carroll Shelby provided it in abundance. Functional rear scoops in place of fakes, and plexiglass rear quarter windows instead of the standard 'Stang's air extractor louvers help identify a fast Shelby.

SPECIFICATIONS 1966–68

No.	Model	Year production		
		1966	1967	1968
63A	Fastback, standard	27,809	53,651	33,585
63B	Fastback, deluxe	7,889	17,391	7,661
63C	Fastback, bench seats	—	—	1,079
63D	Fastback, del. bench seats	—	—	256
65A	Hardtop, standard	422,416	325,853	233,472
65B	Hardtop, deluxe	55,938	22,228	9,009
65C	Hardtop, bench seats	21,397	8,190	6,113
65D	Hardtop, del. bench seats	—	—	853
76A	Convertible, standard	56,409	38,751	22,037
76B	Convertible, deluxe	12,520	4,848	3,339
76C	Convertible, bench seats	3,190	1,209	—
	TOTAL	607,568	472,121	317,404

Prices/Weights			
Models	1966	1967	1968
01 hardtop, 6	$2,416/2,488	$2,461/2,568	$2,602/2,635
03 convertible, 6	$2,653/2,650	$2,698/2,738	$2,814/2,745
02 fastback, 6	$2,607/2,519	$2,592/2,605	$2,712/2,659

General Specifications	1966	1967	1968
Wheelbase:	108.0	108.0	108.0
Overall length:	181.6	183.6	183.6
Overall width:	68.2	70.9	70.9
Standard Trans.:	3 speed manual	3 speed manual	3 speed manual
Optional Trans.:	4 speed manual 3 speed automatic	4 speed manual 3 speed automatic	4 speed manual 3 speed automatic

Engine Availability			1966	1967	1968
Type	CID	HP			
I6	200	120	Standard	Standard	—
I6	200	115	—	—	Standard
V8	289	195/200	Optional	Optional	Optional
V8	289	225	Optional	Optional	—
V8	289	271	Optional	Optional	—
V8	302	230	—	—	Optional
V8	390	320/325	—	Optional	Optional
V8	427	390	—	—	Optional

These and previous pages: a 1966 Shelby GT 350H. The "H" stands for Hertz, the Rent-a-Car company, who ordered 936 of the dressed up GT 350s. Most of the Hertz Shelbys were black and gold, but a few were red, and other colors were also made. The scoops in the hood (top right) and rear fender (right) really work, the latter helping to cool the drum brakes. In an effort to lighten cars, Shelby engineers installed fiberglass hood, trunk and scoops. Center right: the decal immediately identified a rental car. Facing page bottom: the view most people had of this long-limbed fastback. Today, the GT 350H is a rare and sought-after collector's item.

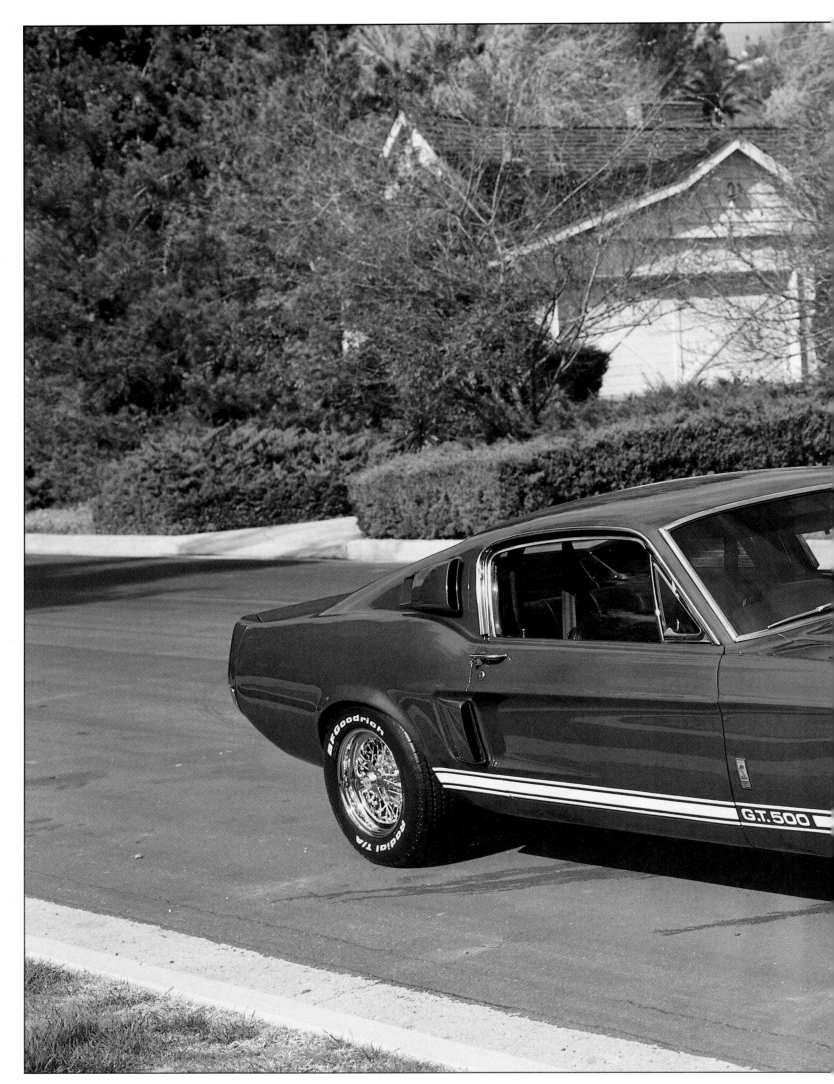

Single headlights were set further back than the grille, thereby enhancing the slightly aggresive stance of these early Mustangs. Mounted almost flush with the front body panels, the bumpers were anything but aggressive, their slender contours suggesting little more than decorative use – a two-mile-an-hour shunt and that bumper would be about as protective as a piece of balsa wood on a NASCAR racer.

The inside of the 1964½ Mustang was as tasteful as the outside. Several trim options were available, with a choice of five vinyl interior colors. Bucket seats were standard, although the buyer could order a front bench at extra cost! Introduced the following March was the Interior Decor Group option featuring an extremely attractive combination of colors and style. Most noticeable was the galloping pony insert on the seats, earning it the nickname of "Pony" interior.

Instrumentation was lifted almost intact from the Falcon, but the chrome bezels were of Mylar plastic and unique to Mustang. A Rally Pac consisting of two black, round pods containing a tachometer and clock was a fancy option set just above the steering column. A silly piece of nonsense were the racing-style holes on the steering wheel's three center spokes, except that they weren't holes at all, just flat indentations painted black. This was supposed to add to the sporty look, although why real holes weren't drilled is baffling.

To further add to the sports image, would-be racers

The 1967 Shelby (these and previous pages) was quite a departure from normal Mustang styling. Fiberglass nose section, hood and trunk tailpiece, together with a different grille, divorced the Shelby GT 500 from the standard Mustang. Driving lights in the center of grille (facing page top) denote this car is an early model. Bottom right: An 8,000 rpm tach, 140 mph speedometer and wood rim steering wheel with perforated spokes set the 500's interior apart from the crowd.

found all transmission shifters sticking out of the floor. That's how they used to do it until somebody thought of the steering column shift. Floor shifts have a nicer feel coupled with the security of being in control; a great advantage, not only to Hot Rod Sam but for the normal, everyday driver as well.

Of the two available body styles, the convertible was the most attractive, and it was only a couple of hundred dollars or so more expensive than the coupé. A little over 100,000 convertibles were sold in the first 16 months, mostly in America's sun belt areas, where fine weather offers the attraction of 'year-round open top motoring. This is not to say the notchback (coupé) wasn't appealing, however. It was, and the fact that something like 465,000 were sold over the same 16-month period shows just how popular it was.

Road tests on the Mustang were either enthusiastic or ho-hum. Most reviews expressed a disappointment with the car's technology, particularly *Motor Trend,* who described it as "a nice looking Falcon." *Road and Track* likened the Mustang to British sports cars such as the MG-B and Triumph, but *Car and Driver* generously described it as "the best thing to come out of Dearborn since the 1932 V8 Model B roadster." As for *Car Life,* well, it really went out on a limb, heralding the Mustang as the "culmination, the sum total of 35 years of development, executed with an awareness of the proper order of motoring requirements."

Top left: taillights from the '67 Cougar were another styling difference between the GT 500 and other Mustangs. Shelby Mustangs were also three inches longer than standard models thanks to the extended front end. Facing page: a functional scoop that helped ventilate the interior. Fitted with the muscular 428 cid, Shelby produced 2,050 of these potent machines.

To be honest, a standard 1965 Mustang used very basic, crude technology that obviously did not cost very much to apply. It had a 55/45 weight distribution (with the 289 V8, that is), a softly sprung live rear axle, drum brakes that forgot they had a job to do after a couple of stabs at the pedal, and too slow steering. The Mustang may have *looked* like a sports car, but it was a sheep in wolf's clothing. Come to think of it, Ford never did promote Mustang as a sports car anyway.

You could make it like one though.

With the right options – a 289 V8, air conditioning, power disc brakes, limited slip differential, handling package, power steering, four-speed manual transmission, 6.95 x 14 tires and knock off hubs – a Mustang came into its own. Sports minded drivers would have thrown away the bias-ply tires in favor of Pirelli or Michelin radials for even better road manners.

Whatever one says about the Mustang, it was an ingenious exercise in car marketing. It found a niche that hasn't dried up to this day. Basic, yes, but then so were a number of British sportscars – true sportscars that thought themselves so superior that soon everyone believed they were.

Wherever you looked there was a Mustang. Only one month after production, Mustang was at the Indianapolis Speedway as the Indy 500 Official Pace Car, and on screen a Mustang convertible was driven by Anouk Aimee's racing driver lover in the classic French movie, *A Man and a Woman.*

In September, 1964, a 2+2 Mustang fastback was announced along with the new engines previously described. A lot of people consider the fastback the most attractive of all Mustangs. This is as maybe, but certainly the fastback roof line, with its air extractors in the upper quarter panel, provides a meaner, more aggressive look.

As a practical four person carrier the Mustang remained hopeless for all but the smallest passengers, although with the skimpy rear seat folded it became a mini station wagon.

Ford celebrated Mustang's first anniversary with two new options. One was the "Interior Decor Group" already described, the other, more important option was the "GT Equipment Group." This was a list of performance extras, already available singly, offered under one heading, and was a mandatory option if you wanted the appearance items, including lower body stripe, GT emblem and fog lamps set either side of the pony and corral in the grille.

At the same time as genuine factory-built GTs were rolling off the assembly lines, Ford took out full page advertisements encouraging the existing Mustang owner to "Make your Mustang a GT! Your Ford dealer has the goods!" Dealers did, too. An owner could buy appearance items and turn his 200 cid six-cylinder-powered notchback into a GT, and unless you knew where to look, you wouldn't have known it from the real thing!

Late autumn 1964. Sated with the Mustang's success, Ford looked around for ways to further improve its good image. Dearborn's number one employer did not have to look far; the answer was already there in the guise of Total Performance. When Iacocca banished Ford's anemic image in favor of Total Performance in 1962, Galaxies were out there winning on NASCAR's oval tracks, Falcons were

The California Special (these and previous pages) was a one-year-only promotional model to help flagging sales in the Golden State. It came as a notchback only, but borrowed a few ideas from the Shelby, including the rear scoops (right), which were non-functional, with the letters "GT/CS" emblazoned on them – CS standing for California Special. Bottom left: taillights are carbon copies of '68 Shelbys. Below: rear has a stripe extending round top edge of the spoiler. Facing page bottom: engine choice on the CS was mostly 289, but bigger V8s were available. Standard engine was the 200-cubic-inch six.

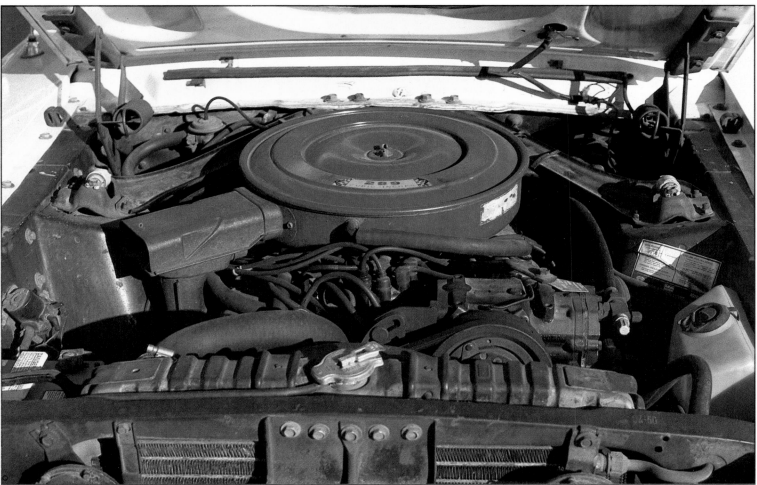

plundering sacred European arenas, and then there was the racing GT-40. True, it had not finished Le Mans yet, nor any other race for that matter, but time would tell. What then, to do with the 'Stang?

America's only true sports car, Chevrolet's Corvette Stingray was making quite a name for itself on the prestigious Sports Car Club of America circuits. And winning. Only one car bothered the Corvettes. British bodied, with American Ford engines and underpinnings, Carroll Shelby's Cobras blew Corvettes into the weeds almost every time they met. In 1963 Corvette's new Stingray was completely outclassed by Cobras in SCCA events. The same occurred in 1964 and 1965. Ford executives watched Shelby with great interest. Hadn't Ford helped him when he needed an engine for the AC bodies arriving at his little Californian workshops? This was true, but it was Shelby, the former chicken farmer and ex racing driver, who had convinced Ford the project was worth getting into.

Ford engines could obviously win races when they were matched with the right combination of parts. Thoughts materialized in Ford's studios, offices and boardrooms: what if Carroll Shelby turned the Mustang into a racer to beat the Corvettes at SCCA?

So Shelby took delivery of 100 Mustangs at his new Venice, California plant. The cars had to be ready by January 1st, 1965, to allow them to be homologated as a production class vehicle in readiness for the 1965 SCCA racing season.

Assembled at Ford's San Jose plant, the cars made the

Below: "California Special" script identifies this special model. Side marker lights and reflectors made their first appearance in deference to government safety rulings. Notchback C-pillar (bottom) is nicely shaped. Right: by 1968 Mustang instrument panel had matured, and was now very legible and good looking. Steering wheel is padded and collapses in event of collision.

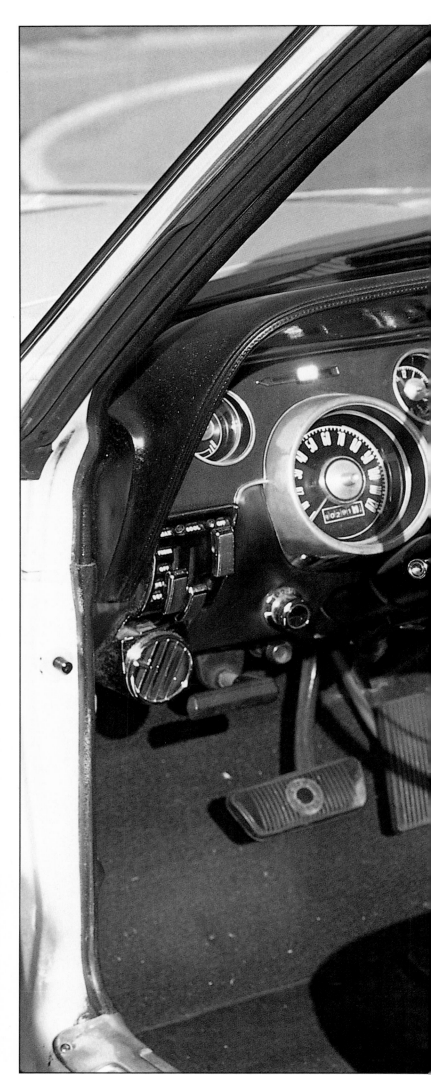

journey to Carroll Shelby's factory without grilles, hoods or rear seats, and they were all white with black interiors. When they left Shelby's workshops these Mustangs had been transformed into a totally different breed of car.

Shelby's engineers started by relocating the inner pivots for the upper suspension arms. This alone allowed flatter, more controlled cornering. A thicker anti-roll bar was installed and traction bars were attached to the rear axle pad. Double-acting shock absorbers were thrown in for good measure.

As for the engines, these were completely torn down and numerous modifications carried out. Once Shelby had worked his magic, the original 271/289 had increased its horsepower to 285 in street trim, and a great deal more for the thirty-seven cars specially prepared for the SCCA championships – these developed between 340 and 360 bhp.

The body and interior also underwent considerable modification. A fiberglass hood replaced the all-steel one and was held down by racing pull-pins. Twin blue racing stripes were painted down the center of the whole car and another stripe decorated the rocker panels. At the front of the rocker panel stripe the letters and numbers "GT-350" told the world this car was more than just another Mustang.

Three-inch-wide safety belts, wood-rimmed steering wheel, electric tachometer and an oil pressure gauge were added, and a fiberglass cover replaced the back seat, the space taken up with a spare tire. Optional equipment was limited, but a racing-approved roll-bar was available if required.

This 1968 Shelby GT350 (these and previous pages) is completely original and has been owned by the same lady since new. "SNK CHMR" license adds a nice touch. The front end is all fiberglass, as is the hood. Bottom: apart from the Stewart Warner gauges, the interior is stock Mustang.

Quite a number of people, including magazine writers, considered the $4,600 a high price to pay for Shelby's GT-350, and criticism was to the effect that the GT-350 rode like a truck. Nobody, certainly not Shelby, ever pretended the GT-350 was a boulevard cruiser: it was built for people who like to drive, and maybe even race at weekends.

By January 1st, 1965, 100 Shelby Mustang GT-350s had been built in time for the car to be homologated for racing in the upcoming SCCA season. On January 27th it was unveiled to the public, who brought 562 of them before year's end. To facilitate production Shelby leased a converted aircraft hanger alongside Los Angeles International Airport, leaving his Venice plant to concentrate on the racing and specialty end of the operation.

As far as Ford was concerned, Shelby had come through with flying colors. Out on the SCCA tracks Shelby Mustangs tarnished Corvette's reputation, winning the SCCA crown three seasons in a row. Just as Ford had hoped, Mustang's image did well out of the Shelby connection, and would continue to do well as time went on.

Not wishing to spoil a good thing, especially with no real competition in sight, Ford left the 1966 Mustang virtually unchanged. Only the grille and the simulated airscoop ahead of the rear wheels were modified, the former losing the bars flanking the pony and corral, the latter getting three chrome bars. Another change was the addition of a strip of bright metal trim along the leading edge of the hood; in 1965 this had been reserved for the GT model only. Also picked up from the 1965 GT was the five-dial instrument panel, which was standard on all 1966 models.

Power teams remained as before, from the 200 cid six-cylinder to the 289 cid high performance V8. However, there was one variation for 1966: Ford decided to celebrate the millionth Mustang by offering, for a short time only, a special limited edition hardtop called the Sprint 200.

Apart from a chrome air cleaner with a "Mustang Powered Sprint 200" decal attached, the car was mechanically identical to any other six-cylinder Mustang. What it had was various option groups as standard – in essence, a dressed up Mustang at a bargain price.

Over in California Shelby could barely keep up with the demand. Everything he touched seemed to turn to gold, his string of successes including the meaty Cobra, the SCCA-winning Mustangs and perhaps the greatest triumph of all, the construction of two of the three GT-40s that won the 24-hour Le Mans endurance race. All this struck a chord in the public's mind, and they wanted a share of the action.

Two thousand three hundred and eighty Shelby GT-350s were built in 1966. Of these, 936 were specially built as rental cars for Hertz. A few differences set them apart from the "normal" GT-350s, such as gold racing stripes and the letter "H" after the GT-350 framed in the rocker stripe. Most of the cars were black, but other colors were produced. Much sought after today, these Hertz Shelbys are quite rare and very highly priced.

A little-known Shelby option introduced that year was a Paxton supercharger kit. It found few buyers at $670, and as far as it is known only 150 Shelbys had the kit installed by dealers and a couple more were fitted by the factory. In standard form the Shelby GT-350s were pretty fast; just

Top right: the 350's functioning air extractor scoop. Right: console-mounted Stewart Warner pressure and ampere gauges. Facing page top: Thunderbird sequential tail and turn signal lights replaced the earlier Cougar ones.

imagine what they would be like supercharged, with the claimed horsepower boosted by forty-six per cent over the standard models.

Although sales remained at heady levels during 1966, Ford decided not to rest on their laurels for too long. By year's end 607,568 Mustangs had been produced compared with a combined total of around 200,000 Pontiac GTOs, Corvair Monzas, and Plymouth Barracudas, none of which were true pony cars. So why worry? Well, for one thing, sister division Mercury had the audacity to declare that it was launching a luxurious kissin' cousin, the Cougar, for 1967. Talk about treachery!

Treachery north of the divide was acceptable – and expected. Spies told of the frenzied activity in two camps. Chevrolet and Pontiac were both up to something and that something was direct competition to Mustang. As for Chrysler, well, it was changing the Barracuda from a pumpkin into a real beauty. In readiness for this onslaught, Ford restyled its pony, added a bigger engine, a tilt steering wheel option and air conditioner vents and controls were set into the instrument panel rather than hanging in the center as before.

What restyling was done was evolutionary rather than

Midway through 1968, the Shelby GT500 was dropped and replaced by the Shelby GT500 KR (these and previous pages). The new car came with Ford's brand new 428 Cobra Jet V8, which replaced the 428 Police Interceptor engine used in the GT500. Like on all Shelbys, the KR's scoops (right) were fully functional. Below: the interior is basic Mustang, with the exception of console-mounted Stewart Warner gauges.

revolutionary. The car retained the classic look of the 64½ to '66 Mustang and could not be mistaken for anything else. Certain changes were a vast improvement, such as the frontal area with its larger grille and cleaned up headlight area, which now looked less like a Lego kit.

Iacocca's original specifications called for an overall length of 180 inches. When the 1964½–1965 Mustang was introduced it was 181.6 inches long sitting on a 108 inch wheelbase. For 1967 overall length was stretched by 2 inches, although the wheelbase remained unaltered. In those days American auto makers still thought that bigger was better, so a couple more inches or so was all to the good. Other revisions included more-pronounced side sculpturing, with fancier twin scoops ahead of the rear wheels. The scoops were phoney of course, for reasons people seem at a loss to explain, although these at least were color keyed, in contrast to the cheap, tinsel-looking add-ons of former years.

The interior was much improved, and refinements included a better-looking instrument layout containing two large pods straddling the steering column, with three smaller ones above them. These contained complete

Macho styling and big block V8 made the KR a mean machine indeed! Due to the limited number of KRs made, they are much desired and command record prices today.

gauges such as fuel, clock (if ordered), temperature, a speedometer calibrated to 140mph and a tachometer. The tach was optional; if it wasn't ordered, the larger right-hand pod contained oil pressure and ommeter gauges, but if the tachometer was fitted then these were substituted by warning lights.

A color-keyed steering wheel had a unique safety

A major restyle came with the 1969 Mustangs, along with several new models. The BOSS 302 (these and previous pages) was one of these. Top left: sports slats mounted on the rear window. Center left: pedals show this car has four-speed manual. Left: taillight lenses are attractive, sticking out further than before. Above: the BOSS 302 4V engine, homologated for the serious business of Trans-Am racing. This car was the best-balanced Mustang of all, from 1964½ to 1973.

padded center hub within the deeply dished chrome spokes which still carried those tiresome simulated "racing" holes – the only thing to mar an otherwise delightful interior. An interesting variation to play with was the new luxury Tilt-Away steering wheel option. It could be tilted to nine different positions, and moved out of the way automatically once the door was opened.

As in previous years, the option list allowed the buyer to tailor his car any way he wanted. One of the most popular options was the GT Equipment Group. With this the car was transformed from spinster Auntie Myrtle's Sunday School cruiser into a man-eater! As the 1967 brochure says, "… wonderful things happen."

Among the extras that tempted the buyers were the four-inch fog lamps built into the grille, wide-oval tires and power front disc brakes, while a Special Handling Package included higher rated springs and shocks and heavier anti-roll bar. Even better, the Competition Handling Package offered, among other things, adjustable shocks, a 3.25 rear axle and limited-slip differential. To really make it go, the big 390-cubic-inch "Thunderbird Special" developing 320 horsepower was the obvious choice. Such was the ferocious power of this monster that it really needed the Competition Package to tame it in terms of handling.

To finish off the GT-equipped Mustang, a nice touch would have been the Interior Decor Group. This included brushed aluminum door panel inserts, brushed aluminum panel appliques and a roof console with twin map lights and switches. With the "GT-A" (for Cruise-O-Matic) accent stripes and bright metal rocker panel moldings added the buyer had an attractive, roadable car at a fraction of the price of an equivalent European vehicle. The GT-A option was only around for one year; in 1968 it was deleted even though the GT version remained. Because of its short life, the GT-A is quite scarce and consequently highly desirable, especially with the lush interior.

Another interesting 1967 model was a mid-year special order option. In 1966, *Playboy* magazine had several Mustangs sprayed "Playboy Pink" for promotional use. Oddly, quite a lot of folk liked this color and made enquiries about it. To satisfy demand Ford, offered the color as an option. All the cars were convertibles powered by 289 V8s and were automatics.

Except two of them.

For some reason, the two renegades that left the factory in Playboy Pink had four-speed manual transmissions and the 320 hp 390 cubic inch V8. It is now known what happened to the cars: one went to Hawaii and ended up a wreck; the other still survives somewhere in the Midwest. As Mustangs go, the "Playboy" is a very desirable car. It did not appear in 1968, although Ford offered a "Playboy" Mustang in 1969. Again pink, this Mustang, besides being a convertible, had a rumble seat where the trunk used to be. Not too many were made and it is another very desirable car.

With sixteen exterior colors, from candyapple red to lime gold, numerous interior combinations, thirteen engine-transmission combinations (actually five engines, each offered with a choice of transmission) Mustang looked well-equipped to face the competitors' offensive. Not that anybody needed to worry in the Ford camp; Mustang carried the day, outselling nearest rival Camaro by more than two to one, or 472,121 units against 220,917. In fact, the rivals' combined grand total was 516,902, leaving Mustang only 44,781 short of being overall victor.

When Carroll Shelby first took on Mustang conversions he was still building Cobras. These cars had proved their worth on road and track more than once. First engines in the Cobras were the Ford 260s, and when these dried up Shelby switched to the performance 289. Then in 1965 the tall Texan bundled a 427-cubic-incher under the Cobra's hood. This ferocious engine was much the same as the engines used in the Ford NASCAR racers, while a modified

Below: raked back headlight covers a handsome styling touch. 1969 Mustangs featured dual headlights for the first and last time. Right: Sportsroof design looks overweight and top heavy from above. Note rear spoiler on trunk lid. Whether it helped handling is anybody's guess, but everyone had to have one in 1969!

1969 MUSTANG BOSS 429

version propelled Ford GT40 Mark IVs across the Le Mans finishing line, 1, 2, 3. In Cobra guise, this awesome big block ran 0-60 in four seconds and could top 165 mph.

In 1967 Shelby decided to build an additional Mustang model called the Shelby GT-500, powered by the mighty 427. Some forty-five or so were put together and delivered to special-order customers and selected dealers. Without warning the semi-hemi 427 dried up, so Shelby had no alternative but to switch to the street-smooth 428 that normally powered Galaxies and Thunderbirds. Although not as brutish or as quick as the 427, the 428 was quick enough for the purpose.

Out on the streets there was a revolution going on. It appeared that sporty, muscular cars with macho suspension were all the rage. Chrysler made its racing hemi available to the public in 1966, Ford had the big Galaxie out there and of course there was Pontiac's GTO, Oldsmobile's 4-4-2 and Chevy's street racers. Insurance men dived for the barricades, aghast at what was going on on American roads. Heart pills and psychiatrists' couches became the whining insurance agents' norm as more and more cars boasting 7 liters took over the streets. It was into this rough and tumble environment that Shelby sold a total of 3,225 GT-350s and GT-500s, of which 2,050 were the latter.

1967 was Shelby American's best year to date. The problem was, how many more years would there be? Sadly, the legend came to an end when the last Cobra was built and Ford acquired the name. Work had started enthusiastically enough on the 1968 Shelby Mustangs during the summer of '67, but the optimism did not last long. As we already know, much of the Shelby Mustang's front end was fiberglass and with the sudden shortage that developed in California, supplies dried up. Then North American wanted its hangar back and with no possible chance to renew the lease Carroll Shelby called his California operations to a halt.

1968 Shelby production was moved by Ford to Michigan. Dearborn control was now complete and Carroll Shelby was retained in an advisory capacity. The task of building the '68s went to the A O Smith Company in Livonia, Michigan, a mere ten miles north of Ford's Dearborn headquarters.

Although production had moved north, the design for the 1968 Shelby Mustang had already been completed in California. The front end had a design recognizably different from the standard Mustang, with a large grille opening above and below the front bumper. Set into the grille recess was a pair of rectangular fog lamps. Large, functional twin scoops were positioned at the extreme leading edge of the fiberglass hood, which was held down by the racing-type fasteners, although the normal latch mechanism was retained. Three quarters back along the hood, functional louvers allowed warm air to escape from the engine compartment. For the first time the name "Shelby" was spelled out in chrome letters across the top of the nosepiece.

On the rear quarter panels just ahead of the wheel openings were functional brake air-scoops and on the swept back pillar a roof scoop. The rear deck lid was fiberglass and capped to form an integral spoiler, while

If the BOSS 302 was meant for Trans-Am competition, then the BOSS 429 (these and previous pages) had to be there for more than a joy ride. To homologate the savage semi-hemispherical power plant for NASCAR, Ford widened the Mustang's engine bay and dropped in the engine. It also went into the Torinos, as Ford needed homolgation in time to race the engine at the new Talledega Race Track in 1969. Huge scoop helped the enormous engine to breathe. This hoary Mustang was a tough car, yet its smaller brother, the BOSS 302, could out-handle and out-accelerate it.

1969 MUSTANG BOSS 429

under the Shelby name 1965 Thunderbird sequential lights replaced the Cougar units that had been used a year earlier. A new poised snake motif adorned the front fenders, taking the place of the rectangular emblem used in 1967.

As before, Shelby models consisted of the GT-350 and the GT-500 – the former now with a new 302 cid 4 bbl engine developing 250 hp. Curious things happened on the GT-500 model, however. First of all equipped with a 428-cubic-inch Ford Police Interceptor engine, Ford replaced this with its new 428 Cobra Jet unit halfway through the 1968 model year, renaming the car the "Shelby GT-500KR." The KR suffix, standing for "King of the Road," now appeared on the stripes above the rocker panels. Now that Ford had the rights to the Cobra name, it was featured everywhere one looked: a Cobra aluminum intake, a Cobra air cleaner, and Cobra Le Mans finned aluminum covers. Seems Ford wanted everybody to know this car was a Shelby Cobra and not lose sight of its heritage, either.

Of the 4,450 Shelby's built for 1968 the actual number of 500KRs produced can only be estimated. That the GT-500 outsold the GT-350 2 to 1 is known. Assuming 2,500 GT-500 models were built and that the 500KR took over mid-season, then an estimated 1,250 were produced. It is known, however, that the KR version is by far the most collectible, and worth considerably more than other models.

It was during this period, especially during 1968, that the American motor industry decided to go for broke on raw power. Hang the detractors, hang the insurance boys, we're joining the revolution. Up popped a line of new, dazzling muscle cars with more power than Clark Kent would ever want to be seen around with. Plymouth's Road Runner for instance. There was no pretence about this car. It was a bare bones, big-engined street racer pure and simple. No frills, a taxi cab interior, and more power under the hood than lifted the first men to the moon.

Dodge Coronet Super Bee, Olds 4-4-2, Chevelle 396,

even staid old Buick got into the act with its GS 400. Dodge's sleek new Charger, with a 426 hemi under the hood, would blast them all to kingdom come, given the chance.

Including the new Mustangs.

Ford entered 1968 with a virtually unchanged Mustang, having extensively restyled the year before. Only the grille was slightly modified by dropping the horizontal bars from each side of the traditional horse and corral center motif. Does the reader have a sense of *deja vu*? As for the pony and corral, this had shrunk noticeably over 1967, and would shrink again in 1969.

On April 1st, Ford announced the Cobra Jet Mustang fastback. Essentially Mustang's stock GT fastback bodystyle, this car boasted the huge Cobra Jet V8 under the hood. The idea behind this model was to counter Camaro's recently announced Camaro SS 396 package stuffed with Chevrolet's wild 396 cid V8, which was intended to counter Mustang's 390 unit.

While the 428 CJ fastback would show the Camaro SS 396 a clean pair of heels – or rather wheels – Mustangs were being trounced in the SSCA Sedan Class Championship by Camaro's sharp Z28 powered by a 302 cid V8. Out of twenty-five Trans-Am races over 1968 and 1969, Camaros, mostly prepared by Roger Penske and driven by Mark Donahue, won eighteen of them, thereby collaring the championship two years in a row.

Mustang, rather like Ferrari, kept bringing out odd-ball models that lasted a single season, and 1968 was a supreme

Facing and previous pages: another one of the 859 BOSS 429s made in 1969. The car itself never raced, serving instead as a bed for the engine that did. The racing-style pins in the hood are part of the image. Left: door panels are molded plastic, and the wood veneer is fake, as usual. The BOSS 429 survived into 1970, and a little over 1,300 were made in total. Today, they fetch premium prices a third of the way up the five-figure scale.

example of this curious anomaly. First there was the Sprint. This car popped up in 1966, disappeared, then returned anew in 1968 as an optional package for a Ford promotional "See-The-Light" sale. Six-cylinder versions got GT stripes, full wheel covers and a pop open gas cap, while the V8 model had all that plus GT fog lamps, wide-oval tires and styled wheels (in place of the full covers).

Perhaps the most interesting models for collectors were the California Special and the High Country Special. Available only in hard top form, these cars were promotional vehicles sold only by Southern California and Colorado dealers respectively. The California Special had a blacked out grille minus horse and corral, together with Lucas fog lamps and purely decorative Shelby-style side scoops. Other differences over the standard coupé included a Shelby fiberglass trunk lid, Shelby (Thunderbird) tail lights, spoiler, Mustang's optional louvered hood, standard on the CS, and chrome "California Special" script on the rear fenders. A white stripe extended to the rear quarter panel scoop with the letters "GT/CS" stamped within.

Like their California counterparts, Colorado dealers also got their special Mustang. Identical to the California Special, the High Country Special was the Colorado dealers' promotional limited edition Mustang. Instead of lettering on the fake scoops, the High Country Special featured a two-tone blue shield decal with the Mustang pony etched in gold running against a blue sky across the mountain horizon. Of the two cars, which were available with any engine or interior option desired, the High Country Special is the scarcer of these highly collectible examples.

Aware that the Federal Government was breathing down their necks, the car makers added more emissions and safety controls. In 1968, side marker lights were added to all four corners of the exterior, while inside, thickly padded instrument panels, break away rear view mirrors, collapsible steering colums, and safety door handles were fitted in response to the growing campaign for safer and better cars.

Autumn came and 1969 Mustangs underwent their second major re-styling in two years. Longer by four inches at 187.4 inches overall, yet still on the same 108-inch wheelbase, the new Mustangs had more "nose" than ever before. Two new models now joined the fray: the Grande, a luxury orientated hardtop coupe, and the Mach I, which appealed to those who liked Shelbys but couldn't afford

one. This year the Shelby GT-350 and GT-500 bore even less resemblance to the standard Mustang than ever before.

Scoops, all functional, were everywhere. Five in the hood, two for the front brakes and two for the rear. The front was almost square, with a chrome edge. The black, wire mesh grille had a concentric bright metal frame with a poised Cobra emblem attached to the driver's side of the grille.

At the rear, a black insert bore the name S H E L B Y stretched beneath the rear spoiler lip and another coiled snake nestled on the fastback's rear roof line. And besides the hood, rear trunk lid and nosepiece, the Shelby's front fenders were fiberglass, too.

Actually the Shelby's front is not as attractive as the

standard Mustang's. 1969 grilles were rectangular, V-shaped and made of plastic for the first time. Dual headlights were used for 1969 only, the inner cones set either end of the grille, the outer lights deeply recessed into housings cut back into the front fenders. As for the pony motif, it had shrunk to the size of the ones used on the fenders of earlier models. Two types of non-functional scoops were used,

Top left: the sword-like shape of the 429's hood and scoop. Above: the interior is a feast of plastic wood, even down to the steering wheel rim. This, and the fake holes in steering wheel spokes, seems out of keeping with a car as savage as the BOSS 429.

SCCA'sTrans-Am racing season.

Niceties such as air conditioning and automatic transmission were unavailable in a BOSS 302, which boasted a high output 302 engine rated at 290 horses. A four-speed manual transmission, competition suspension, a 3.50:1 rear axle, unique tape stripes and matte black hood made this Mustang one of the most attractive and best-handling models of all.

Another shocker was the BOSS 429. This model came about because Ford had developed a big block semi-hemispherical V8 to take on Chrysler's hemis at the NASCAR tracks. In order to do this Ford had to build 500 units and sell them to the public. So to enhance Mustang's reputation, Ford squeezed this mammoth block into its pony car which had to have its engine compartment widened either side. This was done by moving the spring towers out an inch.

Other modifications, such as lowering the A-arms one inch, helped compensate a little for the nose-heavy handling the car would display. Although an exotic – perhaps the most exotic – Mustang with its oversized hood scoop, it didn't have the handling or performance of the BOSS 302. As a collectors' car though, the BOSS 429 is highly desired. Between 1969 and 1970 only 1,300 or so were built.

With all this talk of high performance cars, we should not forget Mustang's E model. The E presumably stood for economy, and the package was economical too. It had the Sports Roof body, a low axle ratio, automatic

hardtops and convertibles had a finned air exhaust vent arrangement, while the new Sports Roof body style had a scoop. Both can be found in front of the rear wheel arches.

Of the new models, the GT Equipment Group option was in its final year because Ford had begun to sell option packages as part of a model's standard equipment, as with the Mach I, for instance.

From its matte finish black hood to its aerodynamic Sports Roof, the Mach I looked all business. It was available with any of Ford's larger V8s, from the new 351 2 bbl to the 428 CJ Ram-Air. Mach I models with the Ram-Air sported a new "Shaker" scoop that stuck up through the hood. Work? Of course it worked, as did the racing-type hood pins.

Also new was the wild and woolly BOSS 302. This car was introduced in March, 1969 as a counter to Chevrolet's Camaro Z28. Unlike the Mach I, which came with a host of deluxe options, the BOSS 302 was built to qualify for the

Introduced in 1969, the Grande (these and previous pages) was as different from the BOSS 429 as chalk is from cheese. While the 429 represented brute power, the Grande was the soft and luxurious Mustang. Shown here is the 1970 model. After only one year, dual headlights were banished. In place of the former outer headlight was a cover with two simulated scoops (below).

SPECIFICATIONS
1969–70

No.	Model	Year production 1969	Year production 1970
63A	Fastback, standard	56,022	39,470
63B	Fastback, deluxe	5,958	6,464
63C	Fastback, Mach 1	72,458	40,970
65A	Hardtop, standard	118,613	77,161
65B	Hardtop, deluxe	5,210	5,408
65C	Hardtop, bench seats	4,131	—
65D	Hardtop, del. bench seats	504	—
65E	Hardtop, Grandé	22,182	13,581
76A	Convertible, standard	11,307	6,199
76B	Convertible, deluxe	3,439	1,474
	TOTAL	299,824	190,727

Models		Prices/Weights 1969	Prices/Weights 1970
01	hardtop, 6	$2,635/2,690	$2,721/2,721
02	fastback, 6	$2,635/2,713	$2,771/2,745
03	convertible, 6	$2,849/2,800	$3,025/2,831
04	Grandé, 6	$2,866/2,765	$2,936/2,806
01	hardtop, V8	$2,740/2,906	$2,822/2,923
02	fastback, V8	$2,740/2,930	$2,872/2,947
02	Boss 302, V8	$3,588/3,210	$3,720/3,227
03	convertible, V8	$2,954/3,016	$3,126/3,033
04	Grandé, V8	$2,971/2,981	$3,028/3,008
05	Mach, V8	$3,139/3,175	$3,271/3,240

General Specifications	1969	1970
Wheelbase:	108.0	108.0
Overall length:	187.4	187.4
Overall width:	71.3	71.7
Standard Trans.:	3 speed manual	3 speed manual
Optional Trans.:	4 speed manual 3 speed automatic	4 speed manual 3 speed automatic

Engine Availability			1969	1970
Type	CID	HP		
I6	200	115/120	Standard	Standard
I6	250	155	Optional	Optional
V8	302	220	Standard[a]	Standard[a]
V8	351	250	Optional[b]	Optional[b]
V8	351	290/300	Optional	Optional
V8	390	320	Optional	—
V8	428	335	Optional	Optional
V8	428[c]	335	Optional	Optional
V8	429[d]	375	Optional	Optional

a 290 hp std Boss 302   c with Ram Air
b Std Mach 1   d Boss 429

transmission and a special torque converter. At least it looked little different from its gung-ho brothers and passed more gas pumps than the others dared to!

As Father Time began to draw his mantle across the Sixties he drew it over an extraordinary decade. It had been a decade of civil unrest, political assassination and upheaval as well as meteoric social change. War was raging in Vietnam, student unrest was rife and the establishment was seemingly being challenged by the advocates of Flower Power and Free Love.

As far as Mustang was concerned it was still 1969 and minor styling revisions were introduced. A pair of simulated air scoops replaced Mustang's outer headlights and this effectively made the car far more appealing. Other changes included a broad black stripe flanked by two narrow ones on the Mach I hood in place of the all black version of 1969. The 351 2 bbl continued to be offered as the standard engine, but a choice of two 428 CJs was available. Unique rectangular driving lamps inboard of the headlights gave easy recognition to the Mach I. Both the low production BOSS 302 and BOSS 429 were in their last season.

As for the Shelby, this was the last year as well. Ford had decided there was no need to continue the marque. Shelby had announced the end of his involvement with Ford in

Top left: here's a decal seldom seen. It belongs to the "Mustang Twister Special." Facing page: essentially a Mach I, the 1970 Twister was born of desperation. Mustang sales were slumping in Kansas, so Kansas dealers begged Ford for a special promotional car to boost turnover. And the Twister was the result.

1969 and with so many hot Mustangs to pick from the Shelbys had become redundant. Nobody should ever forget what Shelby did for American motorsport; almost single-handed he had taken on the Europeans and beaten them at their own game. He had brought respect to American sports cars where none had been before.

Although Henry Ford II did not like Lee Iacocca, he had to recognize the tremendous contribution the man had made to the company's success. Gritting his teeth, Ford handed Iacocca the vice-presidency of Ford's entire car and truck group. Although it was generally thought that Iacocca should have been made vice-chairman, old Henry gave that post to Ford corporate president Arjay Miller. Then, in an unprecedented move, he reached out to Pontiac and offered "Bunkie" Knudsen, the architect of Pontiac's return to performance, the vacant post of the Ford presidency. Not surprisingly, Knudsen jumped at the offer.

This all took place in 1968, and once settled in at Ford's, Knudsen persuaded GM stylist Larry Shinoda to come and join him, and between them they set about making the Mustang into a real cruisemobile: big, fat 'n' sassy. Like 1958 all over again.

The results of Shinoda's bigger-than-ever styling appeared in 1971. Oh boy! Length grew to 189.5 inches, width by 2.4 inches to 74.1 inches and wheelbase was stretched by one inch to 109 inches – the first time it had been altered in its entire run. Those measurements may not sound significant, but what a difference they made over earlier models. No longer was the Mustang a pony; rather a fully-fledged cart horse!

Over the past two or three years Mustang sales had been dropping, reaching a trough in 1970, when only 190,727 cars were built. It was hoped that the new styling would reverse the trend away from sports and muscle cars.

Perhaps this was why, in 1970, the Kansas City District dealers approached Ford and begged a special promotional Mustang along the lines of the previous California Special and High Country Special. Ford concurred, and a group of ninety-six special Mach Is, consecutively produced, were made for the dealers. Of these, nine were four-speed manuals powered by the 351C 4V V8, thirty-nine came with automatic and the same engine while twenty-four manuals and twenty-four

Top: the Twister interior is pure Mach I – only the exterior is different. Of the 96 Twisters made, all were painted Grabber Orange. Half the cars had the 428 CJ V8, while the others had the 351 Cleveland. The Twisters were built consecutively on the Mach I line, although they had different numbering. These numbers remain a closely guarded secret to prevent the appearance of fake versions. The rarity of these cars is reflected in their current high market value.

automatics were built with the powerful 428 SCJ V8. This particular model was distinguished by a black stripe along each side and a black tornado-type decal emblazoned with the word "Twister" on the rear fenders.

To date few knew of these cars until an enterprising Mustang enthusiast by the name of Terry Fritts discovered that such a car existed. So far only twenty-five have been located and two now have homes in California. The other twenty-three still reside in Kansas, Oklahoma and neighboring states. All the cars were painted Grabber Orange and had stock black Mach I interiors and trim. Did the Twister help sales? Possibly. We know at least ninety-six Twisters were sold, of which there are probably quite a few waiting to be discovered.

To return to 1971. Shinoda's styling did anything but reverse the downward sales spiral. Production dropped to 149,678 units for the year. 1972 was even worse – at only 125,093 units produced, it was Mustang's worst year to date. As for 1973, there was only a slight improvement, with sales climbing to 134,867 units. Obviously the public gave the "bigger is better" look a raspberry. That, and higher insurance rates, stifling federal interference and rising prices was enough to dissuade anybody from buying a new car.

There were still big engines in Mustang's line-up. With the additional width, Ford was able to offer the race-bred

Top: radio and temperature controls are grouped neatly above the console which houses the automatic transmission selector.
Right: 1970 Mach I features matt black hood stripe and twist type latches. The raised scoop is functional, telling us that this Mach I has the 428 under the hood. The sporty wheel cover was standard on the Mach I, but optional on other models.

429 in place of the discontinued 428 CJ. This 429 should not be be confused with the BOSS 429 – they were quite different, the later engine adopting thin-wall castings like the discontinued 302 and the current 351.

Talking of the 351, this engine was the basis for the BOSS 351 Sports Roof. Around for 1971 only, the 351 4 bbl with the optional Ram-Air package, side stripes, matte black hood and functional scoops was the model to have. Well appointed, good handling – with the performance options – and fast, the BOSS would have been the first choice, followed by the Mach I

As usual, Mustangs came in the three basic bodystyles and had a large complement of engines, from the 250 cid six first introduced as an option in 1969, to five variations of the 351 and three 429s. One 302 was also on the list. Options galore were offered to enable the buyer to tailor the car to his or her own taste.

Considering that the car had undergone a major restyle in 1971, it was wholly understandable that the 1972 Mustangs are almost impossible to distinguish from those of the previous year. Ford decided that rather than change for change's sake, their money would be better spent on developments to satisfy the government's increasingly stringent emissions controls.

Detoxed, detuned, dee everything, that just about sums up Mustang's '72 crop. Only the Mach I was a reminder of

Left: prominent lettering leaves no one in any doubt that this is a Mach I. The gas cap below the trunk lock is of the pop-open variety. Below: the unique driving lights and turn signals peculiar to the 1970 Mach I. Facing page top: the huge 428 CJ nestles under the shaker hood scoop. Facing page bottom: heaps of fake wood was the thing during 1969 and 1970.

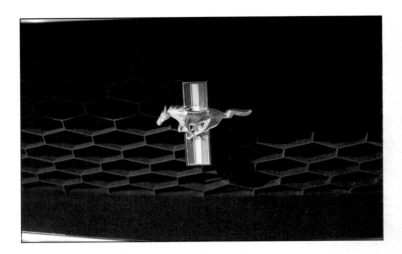

the great performance days, although the 351 was not the engine it had previously been.

In February 1972, Mustang pulled the "Sprint" name out of the bag again. This time the Sports Roof model was white with twin red and blue hood stripes, a blue/red rocker panel and rear panel. Blue was the predominant color, framed by pin striped red. A white and blue interior with color keyed carpet and trim gave the model a rich quality, which partly accounts for its desirability today.

Lee Iacocca was horrified when he saw what Knudsen and Shinoda had done to his "baby." Determined to reduce the Mustang to a smaller, more manageable size again, Iacocca got his way and the new era Mustang would debut for 1974.

Meanwhile, 1973 Mustangs remained as before, with only the grille being changed to an egg crate design. After several years absence the pony galloping in its corral was back in the center of the grille, whilen new, vertical parking lights replaced the '71 horizontal units.

Along with all the other makes, the 1973 Mustang was equipped with new 5 mph impact bumpers in compliance with the Federal Government's safety standards. To make them as attractive as possible, Ford designers wrapped color-keyed, molded urethane around a steel reinforced bumper attached to a pair of shock absorbers. Or something like that. If your car was involved in a 5 mph shunt, your bumper bounced backwards on rubber blocks and popped back unscathed. Nobody thought to ask what would happen if the impact was at 6 mph ....

Unlike some makers who fitted bumpers that looked like battering rams, Ford engineers made an excellent job of designing the Mustang's so they would not look too obtrusive. In fact, they were almost identical to those on the '72 models and blended perfectly with the rest of the car.

The 1973 interior was the same as 1971–72, with very minor refinements. Ever more noticeable was the increasing use of plastics, partly for safety but mostly for economy. Some of these plastic moldings cost only cents to make. No matter how attractive an interior design might be, it is somewhat cheapened by the use of so much plastic.

1973 was the final year – or so everyone thought – for the

At 194.0 inches the 1973 Mustang (these and previous pages) had grown 12½ inches since 1964 and really wasn't sure of its identity any more. Was it supposed to be a sporty car, or had it felt compelled to become an intermediate? More Federal regulations manifested themselves, this time in the form of impact absorbing bumpers covered in colour keyed molded urethane. Bumpers had to withstand 5 mph knocks without damage. 1973 was the final year of the fabulous first generation Mustang and although not the car it once was, the '73 still had presence. Meanwhile, the pony symbol seems to have shrunk still further.

SPECIFICATIONS 1971–73

No.	Model	Year production 1971	1972	1973
63D	Fastback, standard	23,956	15,622	10,820
63R	Fastback, Mach 1	36,499	27,675	35,440
65D	Hardtop, standard	65,696	57,350	51,480
65F	Hardtop, Grandé	17,406	18,045	25,674
76D	Convertible, standard	6,121	6,401	11,853
	TOTAL	149,678	125,093	134,867

Models		Prices/Weights 1971	1972	1973
01	hardtop, 6	$2,911/2,937	$2,729/2,941	$2,760/2,995
02	fastback, 6	$2,973/2,970	$2,786/2,908	$2,820/2,008
03	convertible, 6	$3,227/3,059	$3,015/3,051	$3,102/3,126
04	Grandé, 6	$3,117/2,963	$2,915/2,965	$2,946/3,003
01	hardtop, 6	$3,006/3,026	$2,816/3,025	$2,897/3,085
02	fastback, V8	$3,068/2,993	$2,873/2,995	$2,907/3,098
02	Boss 302, V8	$4,124/3,281	—	—
03	convertible, V8	$3,320/3,145	$3,101/3,147	$3,189/3,216
04	Grandé, V8	$3,212/3,049	$3,002/3,051	$3,088/3,115
05	Mach 1, V8	$3,268/3,220	$3,053/3,046	$3,088/3,115

General Specifications	1971	1972	1973
Wheelbase:	109.0	109.0	109.0
Overall length:	187.5(6) 189.5(8)	190.0	194.0
Overall width:	75.0	75.0	75.0
Standard Trans.:	3 speed manual	3 speed manual	3 speed manual
Optional Trans.:	4 speed manual 3 speed automatic	4 speed manual 3 speed automatic	4 speed manual 3 speed automatic

Engine Availability			1971	1972	1973
Type	CID	HP			
I6	250	145 (gross)[a]	Standard	Standard	Standard
V8	302	210 (gross)[b]	Standard	Standard	Standard
V8	351	240 (gross)	Optional	—	—
V8	351	285 (gross)	Optional	—	—
V8	351	280 (gross)	Optional	—	—
V8	351	330 (gross)	Standard[c]	—	—
V8	429	370 (gross)	Optional	—	—
V8	351	168 (net)	—	Optional	Optional
V8	351	200 (net)	—	Optional	Optional
V8	351	275 (net)	—	Optional	—

a: rated 95hp (net) 1972–73   b: rated 136hp (net) 1972–73   c: Std. Boss 351 only

Mustang convertible, and sales doubled over the previous year to almost 12,000 units.

For the final year of the Mustang that the public had grown to know and love, five engines were available. The 250 six, the 302 which was standard on the Mach I and three versions of the 351, including a Ram-Air option. A Mach I fitted with this engine plus the optional dual Ram Induction NASA scooped hood would give a reasonable showing for itself even if it was a far cry from the earth-shattering Mustangs of old.

One Mustang that did not bother itself about performance was the Grande. As its name implies this one was luxury, pure and simple. First shown in 1969, the Grande came equipped as standard with many of the features that were options on other models. Continuing in its hardtop style, the Grande came with a full vinyl roof in a choice of colors – including ginger – color-keyed dual outside mirrors, deluxe interiors, deluxe wheel covers and a host of other goodies. Performance was not in the Mach I league and neither was the suspension, which was soft enough to go boulevard cruising.

Nine-and-a-half years after its inception the Mustang "died". It had arrived at a time when it was sorely needed and went out when it wasn't. Many mourned the passing of this little pony that liked to have fun and had taught half a decade of other automobiles how to have fun, too.

Top: additional gauges, together with radio and air conditioning controls are neatly housed in center portion of dash. Facing page top: interior is attractive, if a little blasé, looking more like a Buick than a sporty car. Facing page bottom: 351 Cleveland V8 was to be the last Mustang engine with any guts for some time to come.

CHAPTER 2 1974 — 1979

Lee Iacocca wasn't happy – in fact he was downright displeased. Never had he intended for the Mustang to become the dinosaur it now was. Back in 1969 he had known that the crunch was coming and had made up his mind to return to basics; to a smaller size. Late in 1969, accompanied by Hal Sperlich, one of the original Fairlane group, Lee flew to Italy to visit Alejandro de Tomaso at Ghia's world-renowned design studios.

The result of this meeting was the new Mustang.

Two months later the preliminary design arrived for Iacocca's approval. Ghia had followed Iacocca's parameters; the car had a passing resemblance to the 1964½–1966 model. It kept the long hood, short deck theme, albeit in truncated form, and sat on a wheelbase of 96.2 inches.

Iacocca liked what he saw; there was no argument that Ghia's design should be the basis for the Mustang II; now it was up to one of Ford's styling studios to create a design around Ghia's and Iacocca's ideas. Finally Lincoln-Mercury's design team won the day and and although it was a far cry from what had gone before, it was exactly what Iacocca had envisaged.

"Bunkie" Knudsen only lasted nineteen months before Henry Ford II dismissed him, replacing him with Lee Iacocca – the man many thought should have been offered the job in the first place

With the appearance of the new Mustang II Iacocca's judgement and foresight were once more vindicated, for whilst true Mustang enthusiasts may have been disappointed in the new model, it sold like hot cakes. Its final 1974 total was 385,993, almost three times the 1973 figure, and only ten per cent short of the Mustang's first year production.

It was twenty inches shorter, four inches narrower, one inch lower and some 400-500 lbs lighter. Overall length was 175 inches, about six inches less than the 1964½ model. Its grille was not unlike the Mustang's, but was plastic in construction, with rectangular parking lights set at either end. The pony had obviously bolted from his corral because he now galloped wild and free.

Similar side sculpturing to the early Mustang's broke up the rather corpulent profile, which had a lower body molding running end to end. Plastic chrome bezels housed the headlights and the designers tried to re-create the old Mustang's bumper shape into the new, rather awkward urethane design.

Mechanically, the Mustang II was nothing to write home about. It shared a 140-cubic-inch in-line four-cylinder engine with the Pinto. This was rated at 88 hp and was standard on all models except the Mach I, which had a 170-cubic-inch V6 rated at 105 hp. At the rear the large, three section tail lights had European-style amber turn signals that are often considered much safer than the confusing, sometimes hard-to-see red units employed even today on most American cars.

When the Mustang II was created it was based on the same philosophy that had spawned the original. Raiding the parts bin is an ideal way of keeping costs down, and so the Pinto's chassis and suspension as well as the engine were borrowed for the new model.

Both the Mustang II and the Pinto employed unit construction and conventional front suspension consisting of unequal upper and lower arms with coil springs. One

immediate difference, however, was Mustang's lower arm, which was attached to a rubber-mounted subframe. On the Pinto the arm was fastened to the body structure. At the rear, the new Mustang used leaf springs two inches longer than the Pinto's, with staggered shocks for a more controlled ride.

Nobody except *Motor Trend* had called the first Mustang

It came out in 1974 to roars of derision and disappointment from the purists, but the Mustang II sold extremely well, nonetheless. The example shown right and previous pages is a 1978 coupe, the least expensive and most popular model of all the Mustang II's four-year production run. The pony (above) had escaped its corral and had started to grow again, while the interior (right) was plush without being too gaudy.

a Falcon, yet everybody insisted on calling the Mustang II a Pinto – which it really was not.

The 1974 line-up included a hardtop, Ghia, 2+2, and Mach I. Least expensive was the standard two door coupé, listing at $3,134. Weighing something like 2,620 lbs, the little four-cylinder car with a German Ford designed engine (although built in America) had a hard time catching up with its own shadow! 0–60 was achieved in – yawn – 17 seconds, too long to even call this car safe for overtaking.

By contrast the V6 was much better and could propel the 2,778 lb three door hatchback Mach I to over 100 mph. Its 0–60 time was better too, at 13.9 seconds. Bearing in mind the strangling emissions controls used then, the performance was quite respectable, though not in the same league as Britain's agile Capri six.

One area in which the first generation Mustangs were lacking was quality control, which was sketchy to say the least. Iacocca insisted that this be improved with the Mustang II, together with an improvement in the quality of materials used. If nothing else, the Mustang II was certainly well put together, and if it wasn't beautiful, at least it was kinda cute in a lumpy sort of way. It was, after all, an amalgam of different styling ideas. Before the final design was approved, Lincoln-Mercury, Ford, and Ghia stylists put in their ten cents worth. As we said kinda cute....

"Humpy and bumpy", sniffed *Road and Track*, nose in the air. "Mustang is no match for the Capri", wrote the editors of Consumer Guide Auto Test, 1974. Nobody really seemed to like the little car very much, least of all Mustang enthusiasts, who felt cheated and let down – only recently has the Mustang II been recognized by the Mustang Club of America. It's hardly likely Henry Ford or Lee Iacocca cared one whit what the pursuits thought, especially as

Interior of the Ghia had "Wilshire" cloth upholstery, and the Fashion Accessory Package option included, among other things, door pockets, striped upholstery and lighted vanity mirror. The exterior of the notchback had half vinyl roof, Ghia badges, wire wheel covers and pin striping (decals, actually). Taillights in 1978 were similar to the previous year's, although narrower than before.

SPECIFICATIONS
1974-78

No.	Model	1974	1975	1976	1977*	Year production 1978
60F	Standard, 2 door	177,671	85,155	78,508	67,783	81,304
60H	Ghia, 2 door	89,477	52,320	37,515	29,510	34,730
69F	Standard, 3 door	74,799	30,038	62,312	49,161	68,408
69R	Mach 1, 3 door	44,046	21,062	9,232	6,719	7,968
	TOTAL	385,993	188,575	187,567	153,173	192,410

*1977 figures includes vehicles produced as 1978 models but sold as 1977 models.

		Prices/Weights				
Models		1974	1975	1976	1977	1978
02	2 door, 4	$3,134/2,620	$3,529/2,660	$3,525/3,678	$3,702/2,627	$3,731/2,608
03	3 door, 4	$3,328/2,699	$3,818/2,697	$3,781/2,706	$3,901/2,672	$3,975/2,654
04	Ghia 2 door, 4	$3,480/2,886	$3,939/2,704	$3,859/2,729	$4,119/2,667	$4,149/2,646
02	2 door, V6	$3,363/2,689	$3,801/2,775	$3,791/2,756	$3,984/2,750	$3,994/2,705
03	3 door, V8	$3,557/2,768	$4,090/2,812	$4,047/2,784	$4,183/2,795	$4,188/2,751
04	Ghia 2 door, V6	$3,709/2,755	$4,210/2,819	$4,125/2,807	$4,401/2,790	$4,362/2,743
05	Mach 1, V6	$3,674/2,778	$4,188/2,879	$4,209/2,822	$4,332/2,785	$4,430/2,733

General Specifications	1974	1975	1976	1977	1978
Wheelbase:	96.2	96.2	96.2	96.2	96.2
Overall length:	175.0	175.0	175.0	175.0	175.0
Overall width:	70.2	70.2	70.2	70.2	70.2
Standard Trans.:	4 speed manual	4 speed manual	4 speed manual	4 speed manual	4 speed manual
Optional Trans.:	3 speed automatic	3 speed automatic	3 speed automatic	3 speed automatic	3 speed automatic

Engine availability			1974	1975	1976	1977	1978
Type	CID	HP					
I4	140	a	Standard	Standard	Standard	Standard	Standard
V8	171	b	Optional[d]	Optional	Optional	Optional	Optional
V8	302	c	—	Optional	Optional	Optional	Optional

a: rated 85hp 1974; 83hp 1975; 92hp 1976; 89hp 1977; 88hp 1978   c: rated 122hp 1975; 139 hp 1976-78
b: rated 105 hp 1974; 97hp 1975; 103hp 1976; 93hp 1977; 90hp 1978   d: Standard Mach I

year sales of almost 400,000 told a different story.

Nothing was changed in 1975 except the options list, which got bigger now a Silver Metallic Ghia option was offered together with a Silver Normande half vinyl roof. This package came with a cranberry interior and cranberry tape stripes. Although this was a special order limited edition option, any buyer wishing to have something a little different was able to choose from luxury packages, performance packages, vinyl tops and a flip-top moon roof.

Also in 1975, two newsworthy options could be had with Mustang II. Newsworthy because each item is the complete opposite of the other. To help save owners the tiresome business of having to wait in line for gas, the Mustang was given a fuel tank with a capacity of seventeen gallons. At

the other end of the scale, a 302/2V V8 rated at 129 hp was made available for all models. It put blood back into the Mach I's otherwise empty veins and could propel it to 60 mph from a standing start in 10.5 seconds. Compared to the 5 seconds of old, not so good, but great in emission-dogged 1975.

There were no significant changes from 1976 through 1978, only a selection of dress-up kits, go-faster stripes and big, bad snakes splattered across hoods. Having previously bought the rights to the name, Ford offered the public the new Cobra II in 1976. It was quite striking in white with the letters Cobra II emblazoned in white across a thick, blue side stripe. Louvers where the rear side windows would have been, and spoilers front and rear finished off a package that looked as if it should go like crazy. It wasn't bad if optioned out with the 302 V8, but it wouldn't pull the skin off a rice pudding with its standard four banger. Also available in black with gold striping, all the work on the Cobra II was done for Ford by Motortown, a specialist vehicle company near Dearborn.

Smoke tinted t-tops were added to the 1977 option lists for fastback Mustangs only. This semi convertible option package also came with a "basket handle" vinyl roof band – the sort of busy decoration Crown Victorias have today. Luxury interiors and brushed aluminum appliqué on the dash made this car quite stunning in a hedonistic sort of way.

In an effort to give the Mustang II a sporty image, Ford pulled the Cobra name out of mothballs, slapped stripes on the car, tightened up the suspension and threw in a 5.0-liter (302 cid) V8 for good measure. This was the Cobra II, which ran from 1976 to 1978. Even more desirable was the bespoilered King Cobra (these and previous pages) introduced in 1978. Only 500 King Cobras were made, making it the one Mustang II to collect.

1979 MUSTANG "INDY" PACE CAR

Ford discovered that Cobra II models sold extremely well, so production was taken away from Motortown and the cars were built at the Ford plants, where new color combinations were available. Because of the Cobra's popularity, Ford brought out a Mustang II to end all Mustang IIs. This was the 1978 Limited Edition King Cobra, available in either black or red with a large gold and orange Cobra decal flattened across the hood – an idea probably borrowed from the Trans-Am.

Orange pinstriping was everywhere: window frame, belt line, rear window frame, T-bar, from the wheel arches around the whole length of the car and back again. T-tops, sporty aluminum "lacy spoked" wheels, spoilers like you've never seen, air dams everything, the King Cobra had it all!

Under the hood the venerable 302 V8, putting out 139 hp, gave the King Cobra reasonable performance, while the handling suspension, rack and pinion power steering, front disc brakes and Goodrich 70 series radial tires offered better-than-average road manners. Interiors came in one color combination: black, with houndstooth seating areas, the front buckets adjustable for the first time in Mustang's reign.

That reign was almost over, the King Cobra its swan song. Another sporty model for 1978, was a revised Cobra II, its side stripe thicker and running along the center of the body sides, with the name "COBRA" emblazoned the length of the door. A huge racing-style stripe ran the length of the hood, over the roof and across the rear deck. Rear window slats were optional for all models, but more popular with the Cobra Mach I fraternity.

Finally, a special Fashion Accessory Package was offered

All new Mustangs bowed in in 1979 and for the second time in its 15-year existence it was chosen to pace that classic of classic races, the Indianapolis 500. Indy's classic emblem adorns the sides of the Pace Car (these and previous pages). Flat black hood center, silver paint and red and orange striping was attractive, and Ford lost no time in marketing "Indy 500" replica Mustangs. About 11,000 were built.

SPECIFICATIONS 1979

No.	Model		Year production 1979
02	(66B)	Base 2 door	143,382
03	(61R)	Base 3 door	108,758
04	(66H)	Ghia 2 door	48,788
05	(61H)	Ghia 3 door	31,097
		TOTAL	332,025

Models			Price/Weight 1979
02	(66B)	Base 2 door	$4,494/2,530
03	(61R)	Base 3 door	$4,828/2,612
04	(66H)	Ghia 2 door	$5,064/2,648
05	(61H)	Ghia 3 door	$5,216/2,672

General Specifications	1979
Wheelbase:	100.4
Overall length:	179.1
Overall width:	69.1
Standard Trans.:	4 speed manual (4cyl.) 4 speed manual w/overdrive (V6 and V8)
Optional Trans.:	3 speed automatic

Engine Availability			1979
Type	CID	HP	
I4	140	88	Standard
Turbo-4	140	131	Optional
V6	171	109	Optional
I6	200	85	Optional
V8	302	140	Optional

for women buyers. It seemed Ford would do anything to make Mustang II appealing. The package included pinstriping in delicate hues, special cloth seat inserts, a vanity mirror and the aforementioned adjustable seat.

In 1976, final approval was given to the third generation Mustang. Targeted for introduction in 1979, it would be very different from the sad little Mustang II, the orphan in the pack. With its passing, the "there's no substitute for cubic inches" brigade cheered lustily into their Budweiser cans as they eagerly waited to see what the third generation would bring.

"Lee Iacocca Fired." So screamed the newspaper headlines. On July 13, 1978, the man who had brought excitement and respect back to Ford was summarily dismissed by Henry Ford II. To this day nobody has been able to understand why Iacocca, after years of loyal service, after putting Ford's name in lights with the Mustang, was dumped. In his book, *Iacocca, An Autobiography*, Iacocca suggests it was a conflict of personalities and class. That's as may be, but others who worked at Ford during those controversial days say the real reasons have yet to surface. A few know, but they are not saying.

Galloping ponies, graded from black to silver gray (top), were unique. "H.O. Indy" license plate (above left) means "High Output, Indianapolis." Matching colors adorn hood (above and facing page). Facing page bottom: although extensive wind tunnel tests were done to obtain a more aerodynamic shape, recesses around the headlights are obvious air traps.

SPECIFICATIONS 1979–80

No.	Model		Year production 1979
02	(66B)	Base 2 door	143,382
03	(61R)	Base 3 door	108,758
04	(66H)	Ghia 2 door	48,788
05	(61H)	Ghia 3 door	31,097
		TOTAL	332,025

No.	Model		Price/Weight
02	(66B)	Base 2 door	$4,494/2,530
03	(61R)	Base 3 door	$4,828/2,612
04	(66H)	Ghia 2 door	$5,064/2,648
05	(61H)	Ghia 3 door	$5,216/2,672

No.	1980 Models		Prices/Weights
02	(66B)	Base 2 door	$4,884/2,606 lbs
03	(61R)	Base 3 door	$5,194/2,614 lbs
04	(66H)	Ghia 2 door	$5,369/NA
05	(61H)	Ghia 3 door	$5,512/NA

General Specifications	1979
Wheelbase:	100.4
Overall length:	179.1
Overall width:	69.1
Standard Trans.:	4 speed manual (4cyl.) 4 speed manual w/overdrive (V6 and V8)
Optional Trans.:	3 speed automatic

Engine Availability			1979
Type	CID	HP	
I4	140	88	Standard
Turbo-4	140	131	Optional
I6	200	85	Optional
V8	255	117	Optional

General Specifications	1980
Wheelbase:	100.4
Overall length:	179.1
Overall width:	69.1
Standard Trans.:	4 speed manual (4cyl.) 4 speed overdrive manual (6cyl.) 3 speed automatic (8cyl.)
Optional Trans.:	3 speed automatic

Engine Availability			1980
Type	CID	HP	
I4	140	88	Standard
Turbo-4	140	131	Optional
I6	200	85	Optional
V8	255	117	Optional

CHAPTER 3 1979 – 1990

As different from the previous generations as chalk is from cheese, the new Mustang wasn't going to appeal to the macho mob – well, not immediately, anyway. Still, its first year production of 332,025 units had Ford laughing all the way to the bank and not without good reason, for the new Mustang was very handsome, if nothing else.

As before, the new design was selected from various proposals put by Ford's many styling groups. Led by Jack Telnack, executive director of Ford's North American Light Truck & Car Design, the winning team achieved a shape very much in keeping with the then current fad for European design. Certainly the Mercedes influence was clearly evident around the rear window and pillar.

Although the new Mustang shared the upcoming Ford Fairmont/Mercury Zephyr platform, there the similarity ended. Aerodynamic shapes were found to be a great boon to fuel economy, so the Mustang's final design relied a lot upon the results of vigorous wind tunnel testing. There were the anomalies though – like the headlight placing. Dual rectangular light units recessed each side of the black plastic egg crate grille made a mockery of the otherwise backward-slanting front end, this wind-grabbing feature negating the overall aerodynamic advantage. Why flush lamps weren't used is anybody's guess, though the probable culprit was America's antiquated lighting laws.

Mechanically, the third generation car was different, too. Base suspension was the same as that used by the Fairmont/Zephyr compacts: Macpherson struts, coil springs, shocks, and anti-roll bar up front, while the solid rear axle had a four bar link suspension with coils replacing the traditional leaf springs of previous years. A rear anti-roll bar was compulsory only with the V8 models.

As regards engines, the new car offered the same choices as the Mustang II. Top engine was the 140 hp, 302 V8. A German-built 171 cubic inch V6 rated at 109 horses and Ford's snail-paced SOHC 140 cid, 88 hp four made up the threesome. Mindful of its sluggish performance, Ford rectified the situation by offering a turbocharger for those who wanted their fours to scat like a V8. This was the first time in its seventy-six-year history that Ford had ever resorted to turbocharging, and the early results left much to be desired.

Available in only two bodystyles – a two door coupé and three door hatchback in either standard or Ghia trim – the rakish new Mustang sat on a 100.4-inch wheelbase, with an overall length of 179.1 inches, just 4.1 inches longer than the Mustang II. The new car weighed in at 2,530 lbs, rising to 2,672 lbs for a fully loaded Ghia hatchback. Base price was almost exactly double that of the first Mustang, but still a long way away from the roaring inflation that was to hammer the motor industry over the next decade.

Generally favorable reviews greeted the 1979 Mustang, though motoring critics were harsh in their comments on the turbocharged models. Zero to 60 in 11.5 seconds and a 105 mph top speed left the Mustang looking decidedly silly against the likes of VW's Scirocco and other European turbo cars. Another criticism of Ford's turbocharger was the lengthy time lag between acceleration and response. Coupled with a large unreliability factor, Mustang's turbo got off to a very poor start.

Facing page top: shot shows depth of recess around lights. Facing page bottom: rear roofline has strong European influence, no doubt thanks to design chief Jack Telnack, who had recently returned from a stint with Ford of Europe. Telnack was much involved in the development of Ford's European Fiesta model.

Later in 1979 Ford's German-made V6 ran into a supply problem necessitating its replacement with the old 200 cid workhorse, the 85 hp straight six. No stranger to Mustang, the engine may have been short on performance, but when it came to durability it had no peer.

Mid 1979 found Ford hawking the Cobra name again for all it was worth. At least the car didn't look as though it had dropped from the pages of a comic, although the hood didn't escape the flattened reptile! Cobras, flattened or otherwise, only came as a turbo Mustang option and didn't last very long. A one year only car was Mustang's 1979 Indy Pace Car replica. Resplendent in silver and black with red accents, the replica had the handling package and 303 V8 to help it go.

After a successful 1979, Mustang entered the new decade with little change. An optional diamond-grain vinyl carriage roof was offered on the coupé. Ford also signalled its intention to return to motor sports with the showing of the special one-off Mustang IMSA (International Motor Sports Association). Flared wheel wells, a deep front airdam, fat Pirelli tires and flush-mounted headlight covers made no secret of Ford's plans. Later in the year Ford

In 1984 Ford celebrated Mustang's 20th year with a limited edition, specially equipped GT-350 (these and previous pages), of which 5,000 were made. Ford intended the GT-350 designation to remind folks of the great Shelby days; it certainly reminded Shelby alright, but not in the manner Ford expected. Ford had forgotten to clear the title with him. So Carroll Shelby threw a copyright infringement suit at Ford, who eventually settled out of court for an unspecified amount.

SPECIFICATIONS 1981–88

Year	Model	Body type	Description	Production quantity
1981	Standard	66B	2-door sedan	77,458
	Ghia	61H	3-door fastback sedan	14,273
		66H	2-door sedan	13,422
	Sport	61R	3-door fastback sedan	77,399
1982	Standard	66B	2-door sedan	45,316
	Ghia	61H	3-door fastback sedan	9,926
		66H	2-door sedan	5,828
	Sport	61B	3-door fastback sedan	69,348
1983		66B	2-door sedan	56,639
		61B	3-door fastback sedan	64,234
1984		66B	2-door sedan	55,280
		61B	3-door fastback sedan	86,200
1985		66B	2-door sedan	71,891
		61B	3-door fastback sedan	84,623
1986			2-door sedan	106,720
			3-door hatchback	117,690
1987			2-door sedan	64,704
			3-door hatchback	94,441
1988			2-door sedan	85,295
			3-door hatchback	125,930

announced the formation of a new unit. Called Special Vehicles Operations, it was headed by Ford of Europe's former competitions director and was created for the purpose of developing competition machinery. As time would tell, SVO also developed some interesting road cars as well.

In keeping with the Government's Corporate Average Fuel Economy (CAFE) mandate, now at 20 mpg for 1980, Ford "debored" the 302 to 255 ci (4.2 liters). This didn't exactly help performance, but in 1980 who cared?

With the doubling of gasoline prices due to the Iranian oil embargo, powerful cars once again became unfashionable and buyers turned to vastly improved Japanese models. 1980 heralded horror for Detroit and Dearborn as sales plummeted and continued to do so for the next few years. Chrysler Corporation was at the brink of extinction and had hired Lee Iacocca in a last desperate effort to survive. As for Ford, things were not much better. The Dearborn parent kept its head above water only through the help of its European offspring.

For the first time since 1958, Ford division's 1981 sales dropped below one million units. Mustang alone dived 89,000 below 1980's 271,332 total. Apart from optional glass "t-tops," standard reclining back rests for the bucket seats and wider availability for the optional five-speed manual/overdrive gearbox, Mustang remained as before.

1982 was no better on the sales graph – in fact it was decidedly worse. There was, however, good news for Mustang buyers with the reintroduction of the 302. Classed as a high-output engine, the 302 came with a special crankshaft, larger carburettor and a more efficient exhaust system. The only way to have this performance mill was with a four-speed manual transmission. Horsepower was rated at 157 and 0-60 could be rattled off in 7.5–8 seconds. Was this a return to the psychedelic '60s? Not exactly, but after a decade in the slow lane it was a welcome return to excitement behind the wheel. Across the way the new Mustang GT saw third generation Camaros and Firebirds emerge, but in straight comparison tests the GT pipped GM's pony cars by a wide margin in the acceleration stakes.

Missing from Mustang's 1982 line-up was the disappointing turbocharged four. Its lack of reliabilty and poor performance was not what Ford desired at the best of times, and especially not in recession years, and so it was dropped. Apart from what has already been described, the 1982 models changed little in appearance but were given revised model names – or letters to be more precise. Base Mustang was the L, followed in ascending order by the GL, GLX and GT.

From 1983 to date Mustang's looks remained much the same. Hardly surprising considering that Ford stuck to the body introduced in 1979. Rather than the radical yearly changes so favored by the Detroit of old, car companies had eschewed annual restyles for the European method of gradual improvement to a body style expected to serve at least ten years. So, after a decade, Mustang displays rounder, more sporting lines and performance that makes its 1979 counterpart look like an also-ran.

Standout over the past six years had been the welcome return in 1983 of the convertible to the Mustang's ranks. Offered in the top-of-the-line GLX trim only, the convertible was a regular production line automobile, although top and interior installation were carried out by Cars and Concepts of Brighton, Michigan.

Two engines, one brand new, one revised, came into Mustang's life. Introduced in 1982, Ford's first American-made V6 displayed 232 cubic inches (3.8 liters), developed

Euro-influence is strong even if the plastic is American! Tach (above) doesn't seem right with a wimpy 85 mph speedometer, which belies the fact that the car could hit 125 with ease. Nice rear view (facing page top) shows amber turn signals. All US-built cars should have them. The high performance 5.0-liter (302 cid) V8 (facing page bottom) is hard to reach under all the hoses and wires.

112 hp and was lighter than similar GM engines, through the use of aluminum. First offered in Ford's Granada and Thunderbird, the V6 replaced Mustang's elderly straight six as the power plant to have if the standard four wasn't enough and the HO 302 V8 too much! Dropped from the line-up was the 255 cid V8 – all that was available was the HO 302 with horsepower boosted to 175 through the switch to a four- barrel carburettor, high air flow air cleaner, aluminum intake manifold, larger exhaust passages, and other niceties. Remember the troublesome turbocharged four? Well, it was back, this time with Bosch port electronic ignition in place of the old carburettor set up. First offered in Thunderbird's new Turbo Coupé, the engine was available to Mustang buyers later in the year. Speaking of Thunderbird, Ford chose 1983 to swing America into aerodynamically-styled transportation, and the first to be radically designed was the popular personal car. Heavily influenced by Ford's Probe ideas, the new T-Bird sported flowing, clean lines already familiar in Britain and Germany through Ford's aerodynamic Sierra and Granada models. Not to be left out, Mustang was given a more sloped front end with smaller v'eed grille which was claimed to have reduced drag by 2.5 per cent. And to further enhance its aerodynamic commitment, air dragging options such as the carriage roof and hatchback window louvers were no longer made available.

Clever manipulation, model redesign and reduction of wasteful resources helped America's big three automakers through one of their most serious periods since the 1929 crash. Under Lee Iacocca's clever guidance, Chrysler came bouncing back, while Ford's new aerodynamic styling and advances helped bring record profits and sales that went ahead of GM from the middle Eighties. 1983 marked the beginning of the turnaround back to solvency and Ford, especially Ford, was aggressively making the most of it.

Ford ran into problems with one Mustang: a low production option package to celebrate Mustang's 20th birthday. The GT-350 convertible boasted the HO V8, handling and luxury all in one automobile. The trouble was that the GT-350 name belonged to Carroll Shelby and, although Ford had acquired the Cobra nomenclature back in the Sixties, nobody thought about the GT suffix. So Shelby sued. Not wanting involved litigation, Ford settled out of court for an undisclosed sum, and come 1985 the car logo had disappeared from Mustang's flanks. Only 5,000 were produced, giving this car collector status.

Big news in Mustang's camp in 1984 was the SVO, the first real result from Special Vehicles Operations. This came powered by the much re-designed turbo-four now equipped with intercooler which dramatically dropped air temperature to achieve a twenty per cent power boost. Making its very first appearance was an electronic control which could automatically vary the turbo boost at any given situation. A driver-operated selector switch could adjust engine electronics to suit the grade of fuel being used. A five-speed manual with Hurst shifter, all-round disc brakes, Traction Lok differential, 16 x 7 inch cast aluminum wheels shod in Goodyear NCT radials, later P225/50VR16 Goodyear Eagles, tight, responsive rack and pinion power steering, leather Recaro-style seating, a distinctive biplane-

The SVO (these and previous pages) was one of the finest Mustangs of all time. The product of Ford's Special Vehicles Operations, this car had all the attributes of a world class sports coupe. Functional hood scoop delivered air to the intercooler and turbocharged four within. Flush-mounted lights helped the rounded, aerodynamic shape push to speeds above 135 mph. At over $16,000 the car had a limited market, with all but the more sophisticated buyers going for the $6,000 GT V8.

Decklid spoilers (top) add to SVO's European look, while "spats" (left) at the rear-wheel openings helped air flow round the wheels. The radio cassette (above) is Ford's "Premium Sound" system, which makes the driver think he is in the concert hall. Facing page top: the engine in the SVO is the 2.3-liter turbo-charged four-cylinder unit with intercooler. It's not fun to change spark-plugs, though. The interior (facing page bottom) has class, with well-designed leather seats that offer lumbar support and numerous positions to make any driver comfortable. Only 4,508 SVOs were built in 1984, and 5,336 over the following two years. After 1986 the SVO was no more, the victim of consumer ignorance.

With the demise of the SVO, Ford engineers worked hard to make V8 versions as good, if not better. The LX for 1987 (previous pages, these pages and overleaf) could be had with the standard four or six, but was not fun with either, so, like the model above, one really had to equip it with the powerful, fuel-injected 5.0-liter V8 (right). Clean lines eschew spoilers, dams and spats and make the car appealing Top: gone are the amber turn signals featured on the SVO – a retrograde step as regards safety. Above: buttons either side of the steering hub are for cruise control.

hatchback was introduced. Three convertible models were made available in GT or luxury trim.

From 175 bhp in 1984 to 205 in '85 that was the news for the SVO, which became the first Mustang to adopt flush headlights in celebration of the government's new lighting rules. Elsewhere, Mustang's V8-powered GT got a front air dam and small air slot above the bumper. The 5.0-liter GT was a thorn in the SVO's side, mainly because of price and Americans' traditional love affair with the V8. At least sales of the 156,600 Mustangs tempered any disappointment over the slow-selling SVO.

By 1986 Ford was unquestionably leader of the pack, with exciting cars, brilliant styling – the Taurus, Sable, T-Bird and Continental to name but four state-of-the-art automobiles. As for the Mustang, it continued along the same lines as it had done for the previous seven years, with constant improvement and honing of an already fine automobile. A new 200 bhp small block V8 with sequential port electronic injection replaced the carburetted and TB1 V8s. A stronger rear axle and viscous engine mounts (first introduced on the SVO) made up Mustang's important changes.

Rumors abounded around Motown regarding Mustang's future. Ford had joined hands with Mazda and the rumor mill was saying that the next Mustang would be Japanese designed. Mustang enthusiasts went wild, as the number of letters, phone calls and telegrams attested. The cry was

style rear spoiler, a smooth front end without grille, well, these and many other features made the SVO a true sports machine in the best European tradition. Bearing in mind its cost of only $16,000, the SVO bettered many of Europe's sporty cars not only in price but performance and handling as well. The writer personally drove an '85 SVO to 130 mph, and with a 0–60 time of 7.5 seconds only Corvette could come close.

Only 4,000 SVOs were delivered in its premiere year, partly because even $16,000 was a lot of money in American eyes, especially when you could buy a 5-liter V8 Mustang with almost comparable performance for $6,000 less.

Elsewhere Mustangs changed little for 1984; the GL and GLX were merged to become the LX and a base trim

Ponies seem to have disappeared on the '87 LX; a small decal (top) and the name stamped in the bumper (facing page bottom) is the only identification left. Above left: flush-mounted lamps help aerodynamics. Facing page top: interior is sporty, even with standard layout.

the same everywhere: "Mustang is all American – leave it that way or we won't forgive you!" Ford eventually got the message and the new car, built by Mazda for Ford at Flat Rock, Michigan, was called the Probe, and introduced early in 1988.

Speaking of 1987, Mustang's performance king was now the 5.0-liter GT, the SVO sadly dropped because of unforgivable lack of interest. People wanted cubes, and this they got in abundance with the '87 models. Now the GT looked more macho than ever, with flush headlamps, scoops, airdams, and spoilers wherever there was space to stick them on.

In short, the GT was beginning to look like a parody of itself, with a lot of unnecessary add-ons that did nothing for the car's performance. At $18,000 fully loaded, the GT hatchback or convertible wasn't cheap, which made the loss of the SVO as ironic as it was sad.

To be fair, a lot of concentrated effort was put into the GT to make it as good as, if not better than, the SVO. The strong 5.0-liter V8 was given new cylinder heads, which helped add a further twenty-five horses and brought the rating up to 225 at 4,200 rpm. Out went the four-speed manual to be replaced by a five-speed, and those who specified an automatic got a new four-speed in place of the old three-speed transmission. Other improvements included a strengthened rear axle, a new cross-member and the advantage of new front suspension pickup points and fatter tires.

Without its collection of scoops, bumps, and bulges, the Mustang GT could have had a better drag coefficient than its 0.38. Nonetheless, the hard-to-please automobile reviewers raved about the GT – one would expect certain Ann Arbor inhabitants to wax lyrical, but when the staid editors of *Consumer Guide* listed the car as "Best Buy" then the GT must have been good.

Small in number but important to the overall Mustang picture were the efforts of enthusiast Steve Saleen. A builder of competition cars, Saleen decided the third generation Mustang was a good basis for an out-and-out racer if certain improvements were made. The idea would be to sell them should the interest be there. And race them too!

Interest was there alright. From the small beginnings in 1984, Saleen Mustangs now sell like hot cakes. As long as Ford continues to produce Mustangs, Saleen's order book will be filled to overflowing. And for about $5,000 more than a normal GT the buyer gets a racy-looking set of wheels with much improved handling due to lowered suspension, different shocks and narrow tires. Nothing is done to the engine, so performance is on a par with standard Mustangs. Is it worth the extra? That's for the buyer to decide.

With the recession years now just a bad memory, most car makers were cracking up decent sales again, albeit helped not a little by healthy discounts. Ford was enjoying a sales boom that actually had GM worried – as far as overall market penetration went, GM had dropped below forty per cent, mainly due to the better looks, quality and workmanship of the Ford product.

After the re-style of 1987, changes for Mustangs were minimal for '88. Three LX models, the two-door hatchback and two-door convertible led the way with prices starting at $8,726. The flagship was the GT two-door convertible

Somebody had to do it and that person was Steve Saleen. A racer and Mustang enthusiast, Steve felt the mid-Eighties Mustang had racing potential. So he lowered it, replaced the wheels with 16-inch rims (seven inches wide at the front and eight at the rear), and added Koni shocks and other goodies. The result is the Saleen Mustang (these and previous pages). The front end looks like any standard 1988 Mustang with the exception that it sits lower.

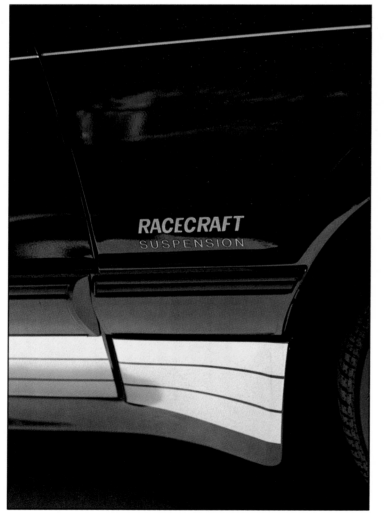

with a base price of $16,610. Cheaper by a little over $4,000 was the three-door hatchback.

While there might be five different body styles, there were only two engines: the SOHC 2.3-liter four and the potent 5.0-liter V8. The four wasn't the turbocharged version – Thunderbird's beautiful Turbo Coupé had that – rather it was the base fuel injected engine with about as much go as a three-legged tortoise. Standard in the GT was the 225 bhp V8, but if the buyer didn't care for all the add-ons and air dams then the LX with the GT's handling package and 5.0-liter engine under the hood had to be the car. It is odd that while all the car magazines laud the GT, nobody ever seems to test a similarly-equipped LX – its better aerodynamics would surely add to the GT's top speed. So all the '88 magazine tests tell of exciting times with the GT. "Still King of the Road" raved *Hot Rod*. Yet a Ten Fastest Cars test in the authoritative *Motor Trend* placed Mustang second from last, three places lower than main rival Chevrolet's Camaro IROC.

1989 was a special year for Mustang. One of the world's most successful cars, Mustang celebrated its 25th anniversary on April 17, 1989. There's talk of a special edition Mustang to celebrate the event but so far nothing has appeared. Instead, the Mustang GT and LX models continued virtually unchanged. The 5.0-liter V8 stayed at 225 bhp, its electronic, sequential multi-port fuel injection system managed by Ford's superb EEC-IV electronic engine

Top: non-standard instrumentation on the Saleen conversion. Left: as the logo says, Saleen Mustangs have much-modified suspension, though its difficult to imagine how an already good system can be improved that much. Facing page top: interior is both practical and attractive. Facing page bottom: rear spoiler is larger than stock Mustang; note the amber turn signals, an example standard Mustangs should follow.

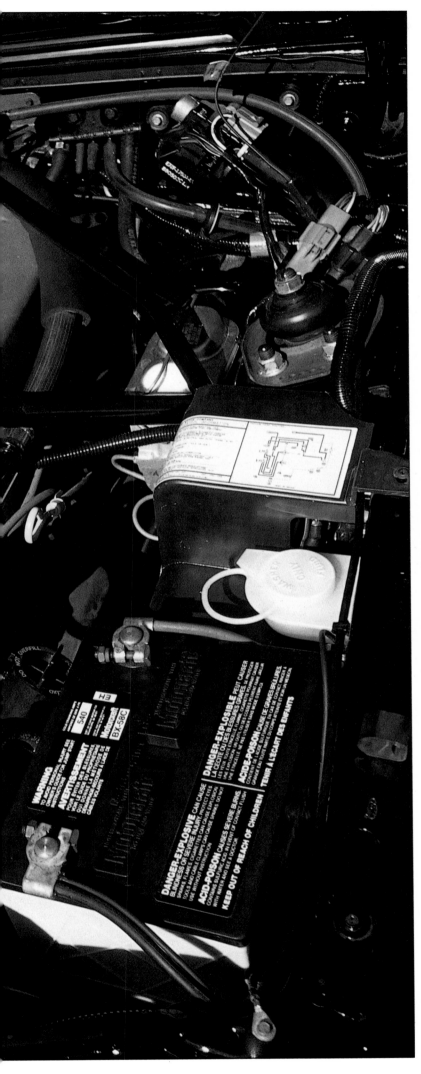

management computer system. In use for a number of years, Ford has improved and refined this system to the point where there is nothing to touch it.

As before, the LX comes standard with the puny 2.3-liter four, but those LX models ordered with the V8 GT package now have their own model designation: LX 5.0L.

Escaping to the sunny climes of a traffic-choked, earthquake-shaken Southern California, I was able to drive both the hatchback and convertible GTs courtesy of Ford's excellent public relations team near Long Beach. Even though the overall squat and aggressively handsome lines are somewhat spoiled by the over eager application of scoops, spoilers, air dams and sills – it brings to mind another era when designers slapped chrome all over 1958 Buicks – the GT has a definite presence that cannot be ignored. There's nothing like it on the road and make no mistake, this car is all go. First came the convertible, equipped with Ford's four-speed automatic transmission, standard power side windows and all the other goodies, such as traction lok axle, leather articulated front seats, premium sound system and P225/60VR15 BSW tires.

No doubt about it, the GT is the sort of car that one does not want to leave. On pressing the pedal the sound of its EFI 5.0-liter HO V8 hints at the performance it can deliver –

Beneath the Saleen's hood, the engine (left) is pure Ford – the same 5.0-liter High Output V8 that powers current GTs. Automatic (top) is the same as standard, but gold-colored wheels (above) are strictly Saleen.

147

1989 MUSTANG 5·0 Litre GT HATCHBACK

the car leaps away like a thoroughbred, eager to show what it can do.

First it was given the chance to show how it would cope with Los Angeles' clogged freeway system, then it was out to the comparative peace of the desert. On the freeways, lane-switching is a pastime to ease one's nerves, and to the GT it seemed like second-nature, its positive rack and pinion steering delivering Ferrari-like responses to a quick flick of the wrist.

Apart from the Corvette, few cars come close to Mustang's handling and road holding. You can barrel through curves with not even a twitch from the rear end – remarkable when you consider its rather crude, shall we say elderly, front engine/rear drive platform introduced over a decade ago. The secret lies with Ford's unique quadra-shock system made up of four nitrogen gas pressurized hydraulic vertical shocks coupled with freon bag horizontal axle dampers. Throw in a stabilizer bar and you have perhaps the most sophisticated suspension ever applied to a system as long in the tooth as this one.

Mulholland Drive is a long climb into the many hills that surround Los Angeles. Rising above the smog one can view the sprawling city and suburbs below. The road is as twisty as an Italian mountain pass, but this Mustang took it all in

These and previous pages: the Mustang 5.0 liter GT, the ultimate American sporty car. Perhaps not as refined as other cars in Ford's stable, it is nevertheless a well-balanced, beautifully handling machine with precise control and high top speed. The console (top) has radio and air conditioning controls above five-speed Borg Warner transmission.

its stride. At all times. it felt absolutely safe, completely controllable and is, without a doubt, one of the finest cars in the world today.

A quick word about the splendid four-speed automatic won't come amiss before looking at the five-speed manual. Through the electronic wizardry in the GT, this automatic shifts in much the same way as an experienced driver would. Step on the gas and the shift is there, instantly. No lag, no hesitation, no hunting. Positive every time, it has at last to be admitted that there's really not much to choose between automatic and manual.

The hatchback had a five-speed manual which performed very precisely and without fuss. While it's nice to throw gears around, buyers in places like Los Angeles would be better off with the automatic. Total price for the very agile, extremely fast hatchback was $14,923. That's the price once a $788 discount has been deducted. It sounds a lot, but where else would you get such performance and handling for this kind of money? Not from Japan anymore, and certainly not Europe.

Nobody seems to know exactly what the future holds for Mustang. In its current form it surely cannot be bettered, and it is undoubtedly the best Mustang yet produced. We are reasonably sure it will continue the way it is for the next three or four years, but we'll just have to wait and see.

Standard Mustang instruments (top) on the GT are non-reflective and easy to read. Left: four-lug wheel is very sporty and handsome to look at. Facing page top: taillights follow current fad for having numerous slots, but the interior (facing page bottom) is practical and businesslike.

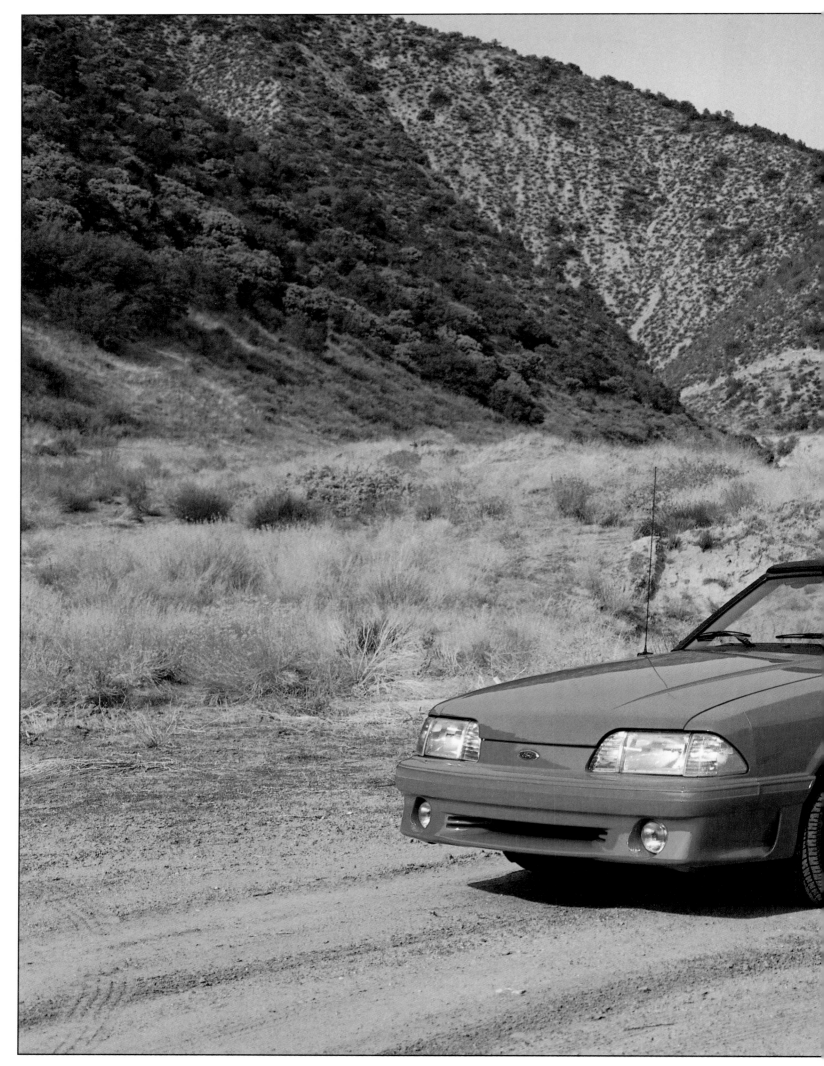

Pictured in the California desert is the handsome 1989 Mustang 5.0 liter GT convertible (these and previous pages). The big rear air dam (above) spoils otherwise good lines. Note how this speedometer (left) goes to 140 mph! Facing page: molded bumper flows smoothly into body contours, the center air slot giving the front a purposeful look. Exterior changes are minimal for 1990, the only real difference will be the inclusion of a driver's airbag to comply with government regulations.

Console (top) looks familiar, having changed little over the past couple of years. Above: exaggerated persepective shows how aerodynamics have evolved since 1979. Right: interior of convertible is comfortable and roomy for front seat passengers, but forget the rear. Overleaf: while enthusiasm continues to grow for the Mustang the sun will never set on what has become an intergral part of American automobile culture.

1970 MUSTANG MACH 1 TWISTER SPECIAL